HANS K. ROETHEL

THE BLUE RIDER

With a Catalog of the works by Kandinsky, Klee,
Macke, Marc, and other Blue Rider artists
in the Municipal Gallery, Munich

PRAEGER PUBLISHERS

NEW YORK · WASHINGTON · LONDON

Published in the United States of America in 1971

Praeger Publishers, Inc.
111 Fourth Avenue, New York, N.Y. 10003, U.S.A.
5 Cromwell Place, London SW 7, England

Originally published as *Der Blaue Reiter*,
1970 by the Städtische Galerie im Lenbachhaus, Munich
Translation © 1971 by Hans K. Roethel und Jean Benjamin

Library of Congress Catalog Card Number: 75-148140
Printed in Germany

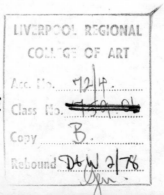

This book is to be returned on or before
the last date stamped below.

CONTENTS

In the early fifties I frequently visited Gabriele Münter in Murnau in order to look at her paintings and to listen to her reminiscences of the old days in Munich. Murnau is something like an oversized village and not quite a town, situated on the Staffelsee, one of those attractive lakes between Munich and the Alps. She lived there in the "Russenhaus," the House of the Russians, which was named for Kandinsky and his Russian colleagues. From 1902 until 1916 "Ella," as she was called by her family, lived with Kandinsky. He had met her in his art school "Phalanx" in Munich, where she had come in order to study painting — women, at that time, not being admitted to the academies in Germany. In 1908 they took an apartment at 36 Ainmillerstrasse in Munich and in 1909 bought the house in Murnau. It is a small house with five rooms. There were no traces of Kandinsky when I first used to go there except for the staircase which he had painted with a decorative motif representing a rider on horseback.[1]

After they separated in 1916 Münter restlessly traveled in Scandinavia and Germany and finally settled down in Murnau in 1930. Some time before, she had met Dr. Johannes Eichner, who wrote an excellent thesis on *Kants Begriff der Erfahrung* (Berlin, 1909), and later turned to art history.[2] He was a man of letters from a well-to-do Berlin family and was able to live independently. Besides being interested in the visual arts he wrote a series of reviews of films during the nineteen-twenties in Berlin and had, moreover, studied psychology. It was he who made "Mü" (as he called Gabriele Münter) settle down in Murnau and thanks to his gentle influence she began to paint again after many years of working somewhat half-heartedly, since her separation from Kandinsky. She used to call Eichner "Eiche"

1 Later I discovered a dressing table decorated by Kandinsky with a man on horseback looking back at a lady on horseback following him. And when I suggested to Münter that this scene probably indicated Kandinsky's relationship to her, she replied: "Oh, no, 'K' never looked back at me."

2 "Das Problem des Gegenstandes in der Kunstgeschichte," in *Festschrift für Alois Riehl*, Halle, 1914.

["Oak"] of all names — he being as tender and graceful as a birch. Eichner and Münter's relationship was a platonic one, based on the deepest mutual respect and admiration. Eichner's book (*Kandinsky und Gabriele Münter. Von Ursprüngen moderner Kunst*, Munich, 1957) is a very reliable and useful source for Kandinsky's as well as Münter's life and work. Last not least, it was the result of his foresight and care that the treasures hidden in the "Russenhaus" survived Nazi persecution as well as the perils of the war.

While I was chief curator at the Bayerische Staatsgemäldesammlungen,[3] Eichner used to come to my office about once every two weeks in order to look up some books and afterwards have a chat with me. On one of those occasions he wanted my advice in the following matter. He told me that he would like to give ten paintings by Kandinsky to a museum in Munich. After all, he said, they were painted in Munich before the First World War and there, it seemed to him, they should have a permanent home. I thought he was joking. After some consideration I suggested that he should not give the paintings to the Staatsgemäldesammlungen at that time because its then current director was a former Nazi who considered all modern art to be "degenerate." Hence my suggestion was to postpone the donation until better times had come. After discussing the matter with Münter, Eichner followed my advice. However, strange as it may seem, I was never shown one single painting or any other work by Kandinsky. So I almost forgot Eichner's story.

In the fall of 1956 I was appointed director of the Städtische Galerie im Lenbachhaus in Munich. Since at that time there were only three early paintings by Franz Marc in the museum, I thought it would be a good idea to try and do something for the Blue Rider group. Remembering then the existence of some ten paintings by Kandinsky in the "Russenhaus," I asked Münter if she would lend me one of them in order to lay some kind of cornerstone for the collection of which I was dreaming. The answer was that she would have to think about it and talk it over with "Eiche." Shortly before Christmas I paid my customary visit to Murnau and the answer was "All or nothing" [*Alles oder gar nichts*].

After lunch Eichner asked me to come with him to the basement. He first stuck an electric wire into a switchboard, unlocked an iron door and there it was: a tiny room with a very low ceiling, apparently crammed with in-

3 that is, Bavarian State Collections for Paintings, comprising the Alte Pinakothek, the Neue Pinakothek, the Neue Staatsgalerie (for modern painting and sculpture) and a number of branch galleries throughout Bavaria.

numerable paintings by Kandinsky. The room measured about four square meters and was filled with wooden racks made to fit the different sizes of the canvases that were stored there. I was breathless. And after having inspected some of the larger formats (it was quite an acrobatic business to handle them) I ran up the flight of stairs, embraced Mü and said something like "But this can't be true!" All she then said very quietly was "I know what I am doing." And this was the only comment that she ever made about her gift, the greatest bequest any German museum has ever received in the twentieth century. It comprises 139 paintings, 282 watercolors and drawings, 226 prints, 24 paintings on glass, and 26 notebooks by Kandinsky. The donation was made public (and partly put on exhibition) on the occasion of the 80th birthday of Gabriele Münter, 19 February 1957.

In addition to the works by Kandinsky, Gabriele Münter donated 25 works by her own hand and also parted with the paintings, watercolors, and drawings that she (or Kandinsky or both) had been given by their artist friends such as Marc, Macke, Jawlensky, Werefkin, Klee, and Kubin. Furthermore, she financed the acquisition of a considerable number of works by the artists of the Blue Rider group. Eichner died in 1958 and Münter died in 1962, leaving her estate to the "Gabriele Münter and Johannes Eichner Foundation," which has since bought and given on loan to the Städtische Galerie the following paintings and one sculpture: Paul Baum, *Village Street*, about 1910; Wladimir von Bechtejeff, *Rossebändiger*, about 1912; Erma Barrera-Bossi, *Portrait of Marianne von Werefkin*, about 1910; Lovis Corinth, *Walchensee by Moonlight*, 1920; Robert Delaunay, *Fenêtre sur la ville*, 1914; Alexej von Jawlensky, *Füssen*, 1905; Paul Klee, *Battlefield*, 1913; *Town R.*, 1919; *The Wild Man*, 1922; *Archangel*, 1938; August Macke, *Three Nudes*, 1910; *Peasant Girl with straw Hat*, 1910; *Garden Gate*, 1914; Franz Marc, *Indersdorf*, 1904; *Panther* (bronze) 1908.

The most outstanding collector of modern art in Germany before World War I was Bernhard Koehler, Sr. in Berlin. In fact, a title that might have been bestowed on him for honorary reasons is "Blue Rider honoris causa." He had started by collecting snuffboxes and paintings by Munich artists of the nineteenth century. But following the instinct and counsel of August Macke (who had married his niece, Elisabeth Gerhardt) and later with the help of his son, Bernhard Koehler, Jr. (who discovered Franz Marc), he began to collect the great French Impressionists, including Cézanne, Seurat, Delaunay, Picasso, and others. He became a close friend of all the Blue Riders, bought their paintings, helped to finance the publication of the famous *Almanach Der Blaue Reiter*, and gave a house in Seefeld on the

Starnberger See to Niestlé and his family. Marc received a monthly stipend from him and, in return, Koehler had first choice in buying Marc's paintings. Thus he acquired the finest collection of works by artists of the Blue Rider group, including about 15 works by Paul Klee and several by Kandinsky. During the last war all the Klee and Kandinsky works were destroyed in the home of the Koehler family in Berlin — a refuge for all lovers of true modern German art during the Nazi regime. Some very important works, such as a large canvas by El Greco and a Cézanne still life, had been deposited in one of the air-raid shelters of the Berlin museums. However, since the occupation of the city by the Russians, no traces of them have been found. All the same, in spite of heavy losses, the Koehler collection remained unique in its kind. In fulfillment of the wishes of her husband, Bernhard Koehler, Jr., Frau Elly Koehler bequeathed almost all the remaining paintings of the Blue Rider group to the Städtische Galerie in 1965.

This book is a translation of the third edition of the Blue Rider Catalog of the Städtische Galerie. The Foreword has been rewritten and has never been published before. The Introduction has been extended. One or two of the passages in the section entitled "Plates and Quotations" have been abbreviated.

In the catalog proper are listed the oil paintings, paintings on glass, watercolors, drawings, prints, sculptures, and other works of art by all those artists who might, in one way or another, be considered Blue Riders. A separate catalog of Kandinsky's watercolors and drawings will probably be published in the spring of 1972. The catalog of Münter's graphic work appeared in 1967 as a publication of the Städtische Galerie; the catalog of Kandinsky's graphic work was published in 1970 (Hans K. Roethel, *Kandinsky — Das graphische Werk,* Cologne, 1970).

In addition to the Blue Riders, there are also listed the works by those artists who were members of the *Neue Künstlervereinigung München,* an association of Munich artists which was founded in 1909 by Kandinsky and others but from which Kandinsky himself, Münter, Marc, and Kubin separated two years later. The reason for the inclusion of these artists is the probability that there will be no special catalog for this group in the forseeable future. And the excuse is that in spite of the artistic differences in principle and in quality, there were personal as well as historic bonds between the two groups.

I am most grateful to Jean Benjamin for all her assistance, specifically in helping to improve my English and to correct the proofs.

H. K. R.

The "Blue Rider" differed in more than one respect from all the other artists' associations founded in various parts of the world from the end of the nineteenth century onwards. To start with, it never was an actual association in the sense of an artistic or commercial organization. After disagreements had arisen within the *Neue Künstlervereinigung München,* founded in 1909, Wassily Kandinsky, Franz Marc, Gabriele Münter, and Alfred Kubin withdrew. Kandinsky and Marc created the "Blue Rider." Actually, what they established was "Die Redaktion der Blaue Reiter," with the idea of editing the *Almanach Der Blaue Reiter* (the Blue Rider Almanac) and also organizing exhibitions. There is no adequate English word for "Redaktion," but one might translate it as "board of editors." At all events, they arranged two exhibitions in Munich, the first at the Thannhauser Gallery in December 1911 and the second (with drawings and prints) at Hans Goltz's gallery in January 1912. The almanac duly appeared in December 1912. These are the bare facts and dates; they hardly convey the artistic and intellectual achievement or the spiritual insight of the editors and their collaborators.

In his concise introduction to the first exhibition, Kandinsky wrote: "In this litte exhibition we are not trying to propagate *one* precise and particular pictorial style; we rather intend to show, by the variety of forms represented, the manifold ways in which the artist manifests his inner desire."

The criterion of selection for this exhibition is not easy to define. There does not seem to be any common denominator in terms of pictorial form. On the one hand there were two naïve figurative paintings by the *Douanier* Rousseau; on the other, the abstract works of Delaunay and Kandinsky. Yet despite the differences between them, despite the variety of styles represented, one common factor was evident throughout the work of all these artists. This common factor stemmed from the nature of their artistic motivation, that "inner desire" which Kandinsky spoke of in his introduction to the catalog just quoted, and which he was later to refer to as "inner necessity."

Once again, then, it was not a particular "style" that united the artists taking part; it was a feeling of kinship with regard to their impulses and the results of their work. But where was the dividing line between, on the one hand, Kandinsky, Marc, Rousseau, Niestlé, and Schönberg, and on the other hand those artists not invited to exhibit? In fact, the choice was based on something like a confession of faith. It was the declaration of a manifesto, the intention behind which was the proclamation of a new and different kind of artistic conception. The international character of the exhibition was not important as such. The fact that the European *avant-garde* was demonstratively united did not represent a move towards an international ideal for its own sake. This was even truer of the second exhibition, which included, among others, Picasso and Braque. The reason for including them was to demonstrate that the search for "modern art" was not restricted to the artists who happened to live in Munich. The idea of "Das neue Bild" (cf. Otto Fischer, *Das Neue Bild,* Munich, 1912) was just as alive in Paris. The *Neue Künstlervereinigung München* had been founded in order to realize this "new painting" through a common effort. In its manifesto, which was reprinted in part in the catalog of their first exhibition, the artists declared: "We presume that the artist, besides gathering impressions from the external world, that is, from nature, is continually experiencing those of an inner world. The search for artistic forms which will express the interpenetration of all these impressions and experiences, forms which must be freed from all secondary aspects in order to be able to give forceful expression to what is essential — the search, in short, for artistic synthesis — is what unifies us in our efforts. This appears to us to be a concept which spiritually unites more and more artists at this moment."

The attempt to realize this synthesis within an artists' union of the old style had proved to be a failure. The withdrawal of Kandinsky and his friends from the *Neue Künstlervereinigung* was therefore symptomatic, historically speaking. If we recall who were the leading painters in the third *Neue Künstlervereinigung* exhibition — which took place after the rupture — it becomes patently clear how wrong Otto Fischer was to cite just those very artists as "protagonists" in his book *Das Neue Bild.* They were — apart from Alexej von Jawlensky and Marianne von Werefkin — Paul Baum, Wladimir Bechtejeff, Erma Barrera-Bossi, Adolf Erbslöh, Pierre Girieud, and Alexander Kanoldt. To the Blue Rider artists their efforts must have appeared somewhat *passé.* The breakaway group no doubt dismissed Girieud's work, with its faintly Pre-Raphaelite flavor, as an outdated form of Nabism, and Bechtejeff's as watered-down Cubism; Erbslöh and Kanoldt they probably rejected — not unjustly, perhaps — as narrow-minded academic sticklers in whom the true flame of reformation did not burn. In terms of form, however, Jawlensky may be considered as belonging to the Blue Riders; and also Marianne von Werefkin, not only because of the naïveté of her narrative paintings but above all because of her manner of thinking and feeling, which was based upon her faith in the art of the future. In 1913, anyway, they both took part in a Blue Rider exhibition organized by Herwarth Walden.

Of course, the contrast between the two exhibiting groups was not as clear at the time as we see it now. However, when the almanac came out it became evident beyond doubt how profoundly different the Blue Riders' conception of art was, and how revolutionary were the very juxtaposition and confrontation of such diverse expressions of the human spirit as Bavarian paintings on glass, late medieval woodcuts, Chinese drawings, paintings by Picasso, children's drawings, graphics by the *Brücke* group, a sculpture from South Borneo, *Biedermeier* book illustrations, the mosaics of St. Mark's in Venice, Russian folk art, Alaskan textiles, and paintings by El Greco, Cézanne, Matisse, van Gogh, and Delaunay. In addition, there were reproductions of the Blue Rider artists' own works, including some by Klee, and music by Schönberg and Anton von Webern; Kandinsky, Marc, Macke, and others contributed essays on the problems of form and presented new ideas about the possibilities of the modern theater. What was the common link between all these contradictory manifestations, what made it possible to speak in the same breath about El Greco and a Bavarian votive, or a child's drawing and a painting by Cézanne? It lay neither in the intellectual nor in the religious domain; it was a matter neither of craftsmanship nor of virtuosity; it was not limited to any particular epoch nor was it tied to any special style. Everything they loved and admired was opposed to traditional easel painting and to all other forms of academicism. In all their "prototypes," and in all their "precursors" from past and present they admired the form born of an "inner necessity," that form which — notwithstanding all the shortcomings and imperfections that might tarnish it — embodied a subjective truth. What the Blue Riders rejected by virtue of their ethos and by virtue of their idealistic sensibility (which was not confined to the realm of esthetics), was what they felt to be the materialistic content and form of Impressionist painting. All of them, in one way or another, had their roots in this tradition, and all of them surpassed it, laying down in their work a new basis for *bildnerisches Denken* [thinking in terms of form] and opening up new possibilities for understanding and interpretation of art in general.

Kandinsky, photographed by Gabriele Münter, 1913

Franz Marc, photographed by Gabriele Münter, 1913

THE BLUE RIDER
IN MODERN GERMAN PAINTING*

"Who wishes to be creative . . . must first blast and destroy accepted values."
However much the truth of these words of Friedrich Nietzsche may be
doubted, they must be accepted on historical grounds as having provided a
beacon for the artistic revolution at the beginning of the twentieth century.
Possessed by a wonderful *élan vital,* the modern artists felt themselves to be
destroyers of the conventions surrounding them, and at the same time augurs
of new and unknown values. This holds true for the *Fauves* and the Cubists
of France as well as for the Futurists of Italy. In Germany it was the members of the *Brücke* and the Blue Rider artists whose achievements provided
the foundations for the development of painting during the last fifty years.
The moderns did not only fight against traditional art forms, a new consciousness formed the basis of their attitude, and they believed that only
in conjunction with the problem of human existence could the artistic problems be solved. As a result the work of art takes on a completely different
importance in relation to life. It is no longer commentary, a window into an
imagined world; it seems to have escaped from traditional esthetic limita-
tions and appears to have gained a directness and an autonomy all of its
own. Robbed of its representative function in religion, expelled from its
secure position within the social hierarchy, it loses its illusionary character
and becomes the direct, personal expression of its creator. It encounters a
new society which is bound neither by sociology nor cult. Almost without
cause, without transition, and without hypocrisy, the new world of color
and form appears, and with what brightness and with what directness is the
beauty of modern painting revealed!

Manet's paintings, and those of the Impressionists, too, were still full of
opposing tensions between the creative artist and the world; they still belong
to the classical sphere of the "representative" arts. The question of "how" in
the reproduction of the motif still takes first place. Cézanne occupies a
unique position.

The new idea, however, that distinguishes all modern art from that of the
past five hundred years is that the mere reproduction of existing objects and
contents is replaced by the creation of pure forms, which, objective or not,

* From Hans Konrad Roethel, *Modern German Painting*, London, 1956.

15

as such, become expressions of beauty. The autonomy of the work of art, however, brings with it a change in the relationship between the spectator and the creation. Arbitrary esthetic pleasure, through the medium of a refined sensitivity for formal values, is replaced by a personal participation provoked by the work of art.

In the chronicle of the *Brücke*, Kirchner said, "With the belief in a development, in a new generation of creators as well as of spectators, we call upon youth to rally, to fight for elbow room and for the right to live our own lives, away from the established older artists. All those belong to us who reproduce, directly and unadulteratedtly, that which urges them to create." This is not an esthetic program, it is no theoretical manifesto, not even an artistic credo in its narrower sense. It is the expression of a new consciousness of life. Artists confronted the anemic intellectualism of a civilization self-complacently preening itself while threatened with suffocation in the materialism of a utilitarian belief in progress, with the belief in a new world, which to them (to quote Nietzsche) still seemed "abundant in beauty, strangeness, doubt, horror, and divinity." Like Zarathustra, they felt themselves "premature children of a yet unproved future." And despite the confusion, contradiction, and desperate need which made their first steps in the new direction so difficult, they were nevertheless convinced that through their work they would "create symbols which could take their place on the altars of the future intellectual religion." When Franz Marc wrote these words in the *Almanach Der Blaue Reiter* he felt himself of one mind with the *avant-gardists* of a new art of expression, to whose representatives, in his opinion, the Italian Futurists belonged just as much as Picasso, Chagall, and the members of the *Brücke*.

The Futurists, with their iconoclastic ideas, had displayed an almost hectic fanaticism. Exciting though their artistic language was, and despite the fact that their cultural criticism must be considered symptomatic of the then European situation, the extremism of their views was not so intimately related to the national temperament as were those of the Expressionists with the German character. The influence of their work was limited. In contrast to this, the aspirations of the *Fauves,* the French "Savages," fused with the great artistic tradition of France, that happy country where even the most savage outsiders still preserve enough *raison* to allow their future inclusion in the spiritual Pantheon of their nation. Let us take Matisse, for example: "What I strive for, above all, is expression." That could just as well have been said by the German Expressionists. But despite the solidarity of their intentions, despite the great similarity even in form, Matisse's art always retained that

16

grain of *contenance* and that decorum that the German "savages" were fated to lose because they cherished more adventurous ambitions. In Germany, however, as has already been mentioned, Expressionism was at first a general term for all non-Impressionist, or more accurately, all anti-Impressionist art; it was retained as a slogan for a long time, not altogether unjustifiably. For in spite of all the differences that have in the meantime become evident, the artists of the *Brücke* and of the Blue Rider still had in common their cultural criticism, their faith in a new world, their rejection of Impressionism, which they considered materialistic, and the vigor with which they strove towards their goal.

The Expressionism of the *Brücke* was in some ways a product of North German Protestantism. The mode of expression used by the members of the Blue Rider, saturated in the spirit of Nietzsche, was based on the same principles, even though their headquarters were in Munich. But however closely related their exordiums might have been, wavering between despair and hope, the artistic results were entirely different. The two groups were united in their renunciation of the "easy enjoyment of a romantic retrospection"; in their rejection of the "vainglorious progressiveness of positivism"; and not last in their resistance against the "rationalistic arrogance and frivolity" and the "mendaciousness of European morale." Their hate was directed especially against the "emptiness of art routine, which isolates the artist just as much as it does the work of art." But whereas the *Brücke* members eruptively produced their passionate work from the depths of primitive emotion, the Blue Rider artists gained, through the speculative efforts of Kandinsky and the religious ethos of Franz Marc, a certain spiritual quality foreign to the other group. The *Brücke* followers did not talk, they painted. Their works are like an outcry. The members of the Blue Rider, however, started from the intellect, they analyzed, philosophized. They were just as much interested in religious questions as in the developments in modern music, in the theater, and in literature. Their curiosity in the startling discoveries of modern natural science, which, of course, they felt rather than considered, convinced them *a priori* that they were pioneering truth-seekers. What they heard about those sciences, actually so remote from them, was not, however, the basis of their work as has been claimed. But as the pioneers of a new world, as they felt themselves to be, they instinctively sensed something of the significance of the scientific revolution. They welcomed these discoveries as confirmation of the fact that the old world which they sought to overthrow was also "scientifically" unsound. Thus the Blue Rider artists were conscious of being on the brink of a dangerous future, and were prepared courageously to carry their share of responsibility. That imparted the glory of young heroes to them: "Many who are not filled with an inner passion will freeze and withdraw to the ruins of their memories" (Franz Marc).

Apart from their artistic aims, and apart from the ethos, the spiritual quality, and their characteristic confidence, the Blue Rider artists differed from the *Brücke* group above all in that they did not pursue a communal existence. Munich, that Janus-faced city, where rural life and cosmopolitanism peacefully mingle, was the meeting ground of those artists, who, varied as they were by background and education, first proclaimed their unity in the *Neue Künstlervereinigung München* and later in the activities of the Blue Rider. During the last decade of the nineteenth century new forces were already stirring, with the result that Munich's fame as a cradle of the arts no longer rested on the legendary era of Ludwig I. The realm of the powerful leading artist, Franz von Lenbach, was considerably shaken by the forming of the *Sezession* in 1893 (the same year in which Thomas Mann moved to Munich). Franz von Stuck, Fritz von Uhde, and Gotthard Kühl were among the leaders of the new group. Arnold Böcklin, Lovis Corinth, Max Liebermann, Max Slevogt, Wilhelm Trübner, and Adolf Hölzel exhibited in the *Sezession's* first show in Prinzregentenstrasse. At the same time Hermann Obrist displayed his embroideries. They were dainty floral ornaments which obviously rejected Renaissance eclecticism: *art nouveau* put forth its first shoots. In 1894 Otto Eckmann had his paintings publicly auctioned. He called them ironically his "artistic legacy." Easel painting in the old style was to be buried once and for all. The magazines *Pan* (1895-1900), the aptly named *Jugend* [Youth], and *Simplicissimus* appeared in Munich (the two latter since 1896). In 1898 August Endell designed his fantastic façade ornament for the Elvira Photographic Studio, and in 1901, Richard Riemerschmid built the Munich Schauspielhaus, which still must be considered one of the most successful theater buildings in the world.

The fermenting atmosphere of Munich during the nineties attracted art-smitten youths from Chicago to Moscow to the banks of the Isar. In 1896 Alexej von Jawlensky came with Marianne von Werefkin; Kandinsky followed in 1897; they studied with Anton Azbé. In 1898 Kubin and Klee arrived. Then Bechtejeff and the Burljuk brothers joined the Russian colony — to mention only the names of the most important artists who joined the intimate circle of the Blue Rider. As has been said before in 1909 Kandinsky, with his Russian friends and Gabriele Münter, Adolf Erbslöh, Alexander Kanoldt, and others, formed the *Neue Künstlervereinigung München.* Their first exhibition took place that winter. A somewhat confused pamphlet issued at the foundation of the group was reprinted in the foreword to the catalog. The group believed that the artist, apart from the impressions he receives from the objective world, should continually be gathering inner experience, and this total experience, freed of all irrelevance, should be formed into a new artistic synthesis. That was an old, romantic tune and a very tame slogan for the painting of the future. Seen in relation to the artistic situation of that time and to later events, it meant the rejection of naturalistic *plein-air* painting, that form of German Impressionism which was cultivated by the *Sezession*. At the second exhibition, held in the following year, Braque, Kees van Dongen, Picasso, Rouault, and Vlaminck appeared as guests. Le Fauconnier and Pierre Paul Girieud had become members. The international flavor was nothing new; it was in keeping with an old tradition of the *Glaspalast*, the famous exhibition hall in Munich. This exhibition, however, provided the first international survey of the new movement. Burljuk in his foreword proclaimed the "spiritual relationship" with Cézanne, Gauguin, van Gogh, Matisse, and Picasso. The "archaic" and the "wonderful fairy-tale world of Scythian plastic art" were evoked; civilized refinement was to be confronted with the naïve. It was felt that greatness of pure form was to be found in the works of the primitives rather than in those of the leading masters of the day. They attacked the adventitious character of their motifs and their unnecessary thoroughness in the execution of details. They missed above all what they called the "spiritual experience," a quality that Kandinsky was later to call "the spiritual in art." In the foreword to the catalog of this exhibition, Kandinsky defined more clearly than in any other of his writings the content and form of his artistic aims — though characteristically with a question mark: "The communication of what is secret by what is secret — is not that the content?" This sentence was to presage future events.

The preparations for the 1911 exhibition led to a split in the *Neue Künstlervereinigung München*. In accordance with the regulations Kandinsky demanded that his works should not be submitted to the jury. As this request was not agreed to, Kandinsky, Münter, Kubin, and Franz Marc withdrew from the group. This step was not the result of hurt ambitious pride, as artists' quarrels so often are. It was both artistically sensible and necessary. At the coffee table at Marc's house in Sindelsdorf, the little storm troop gave itself its name, this name which still appears to be full of yearning and stormy courage: *Der Blaue Reiter* [The Blue Rider]. In fact this name meant only the editorial staff (Kandinsky and Marc) of an art almanac which, as such, published only one volume dedicated to Hugo von Tschudi, 1912, and organized two exhibitions in Munich.

The first exhibition organized by the Blue Rider took place in the Arco-Palais in Munich. It consisted of forty-three pictures and lasted only three weeks. Apart from Kandinsky, Marc, and Münter, works by Burljuk, Macke, Campendonk, and Jean Niestlé were exhibited. Jawlensky and Werefkin, although artistically and personally closely connected with the Blue Rider, did not participate. Among the foreigners represented, Henri Rousseau, who had died the previous year, and the contemporary co-belligerent Delaunay, took first place. Arnold Schönberg, the musician, was also represented by three works. The second exhibition, arranged a few months later (March-April 1912) consisted only of graphic art. All the *Brücke* members were included as well as Klee, Arp, Braque, Derain, Malewitsch, Morgner, Nolde, and Picasso. This exhibition was anything but stylistically consistent; but the *avant-garde* which was everywhere to triumph over nationalism had declared its solidarity.

But what were the artistic results?

The group of Russian artists had brought with them from their remote homeland (which later was to influence Rilke and Barlach so deeply) a strange spiritual ethos. They combined a revolutionary pathos with an introversion of emotions. In 1903 Kandinsky's meeting with the symbolism of the West produced an art of sophisticated fairy-tale illustration; thus, for example in *Poésies sans Paroles*, a popular balladic element is mixed with the conscious curves of an Aubrey Beardsley. In the same period a consolidation of his impressionist technique took place: his patches of color which up till then had been stippled were now formally controlled in the style of Signac and appear slightly sharpened in tone. The motifs, which are mainly landscapes, lack emotional content — it seems as if the artist had to catch up on the course of European painting since Cézanne. In the Murnau period the creative character of his work becomes a law unto itself. A painting of a tree trunk, for example, may still resemble its natural appearance but, at the same time, loses its representational value. The color scale has become an independent element of the picture's organism. In 1909 Kandinsky and Gabriele Münter acquired a house in Murnau; at the same time Jawlensky frequently visited there with Marianne von Werefkin. They all had made themselves acquainted with the state of flux in European painting. But in Murnau, where they could look at the great mountain range, and live so close to the beloved waters of the Staffelsee, in the pleasant foothills of the Bavarian Alps, everything to be learned and sought after seemed to be forgotten. Somewhere in their artistic consciousness memories of Russian folk art encountered Bavarian paintings on glass, which they could still see being painted in the traditional style in Murnau. The colorful dreams of youth unexpectedly came across an ancient practice long perfected. It is true that Matisse influenced them indirectly through his emancipation of color. But these darksome landscapes that were now painted with such verve by Kandinsky, Münter, and Jawlensky are in their naïveté, their brillant freshness, their simplicity and depth, original creations. They opened the path for the Blue Rider. What Kandinsky worked out step by step with much reflection seems to have been achieved with all the force of her naïve self-reliance, almost playfully, by Gabriele Münter in one stroke of genius. Jawlensky's approach had much in common with Münter's. Even he, the former captain of a Russian grenadier regiment, created more freely, was less controlled and complicated than the methodical Kandinsky. Areas of strong and deep color, outlined in black, represent mountains, fields, trees, and houses. The brush technique is fast and relaxed, often refreshingly carefree; the pictures seem improvised, like inspirations of a happy moment. The character of these paintings is determined not by the compact instrumentation of the traditional palette, not by endless nuances of light and shade, the variety of foliage, grass, and branches, but by the harmony of tones independent of sculptural factors, and by an accentuation of the form. It is not true to say that the "essence" of the Bavarian landscape has been given shape by these works just because the artists have succeeded in reducing the multiplicity of the visible world to a few optical formulae. They are pictures that daringly reject naturalistic pictorial representation; their importance lies in their expression of a simple and deep feeling that is reflected in nature. This applies above all to Münter and Jawlensky. Münter had by then found her artistic province, and it was to remain practically unchanged. Jawlensky developed in a strange manner through his contact with the *Bauhaus,* which is reflected in his many variations on two themes — the landscape and the human face. But on closer examination how complicated are Kandinsky's pictures of this early Murnau period! Although his paintings are less emotional than Münter's and Jawlensky's works, less warm and radiant, his color composition is more accomplished and daring. Taut patches of red, in contrast to the dispersed cold green of a tree shape, form here explosive centers of energy. The brush stroke, sometimes stippled, sometimes in controlled parallel lines, is subordinated in length, direction, strength, and liveliness to the organization of the painting. That was inherited straight from Cézanne. One can sense in these pictures the future still fettered, but impatiently striving to free itself.

In addition to the landscapes, Kandinsky also produced, about 1910, a series of pictures which he called *Improvisations*, strange colorful tapestries that tell of riders, cupolas, and women, of swords and goblets; they are like songs without words which express old feelings in new tunes, the content never quite comprehensible, never unequivocally described, iridescent like an old legend. Some pictures from this period, due to their subjects, have a certain sentimental paleness about them, a smack of sophisticated *art nouveau*. One should not lose sight of his earlier subjects when judging the possible content of Kandinsky's later works. Despite their abstract quality they still retain a good proportion of his youthful ideas. However that may be, the formal development seen in its infancy in the *Improvisations* is of great importance for the conquest of a new world of forms. If one tries to define his aims as simply as possible, one might say: tenderness was no longer to be restricted to the genrelike representation of an embrace, nor movement to the concrete portrayal of a dance. The endless realm of spiritual halftones, from the ominous and inarticulate to the robust *tutti furiosi*, was to be given artistic shape through the vibration of color and form. This, however, was no mere logical development or theory such as had been cherished by romantics like Philipp Otto Runge and Novalis. It was a spontaneous and direct approach to art. It needed all Kandinsky's self-devotion to realize what had never been achieved before.

Kandinsky had told Gabriele Münter as early as 1905, long before he had grasped his artistic aims, that even as a student he had already found the subject matter of painting more of a disturbance than a help. The basic conditions necessary for abstract painting had already been created by the color experiments and the work on composition problems of the Neo-Impressionists. Looking back, van Gogh and Seurat had already started to come to grips with these problems that were later to be solved by Kandinsky as a morphological consequence. There had been many concrete attempts in the direction of abstract painting; in Munich, Hölzel had tested artistic mediums for their independent values, though more by way of experiment. Endell had theorized about them. The Munich *Jugendstil* was Kandinsky's most important and at the same time most dangerous forerunner. One only needs to recall the independent power of line as it had been formulated by van de Velde: "A line is a force, borrowing its power from the energy of the draftsman." This provided a fruitful beginning. Nobody was more aware than Kandinsky of the danger of petrifaction at the ornamental stage, and his development quite distinctly shows that he avoided this short circuit inherent in abstract art. Kandinsky himself mentioned the preliminary stages through which he passed: having seen one of Monet's *Haystacks* in Moscow,

22

he unconsciously came to the conclusion that "the object was no longer an inevitable element of a picture." Wagner's *Lohengrin* made a lasting synesthetic impression on him: "I saw all my colors; they stood before my eyes. Wild, almost crazy lines drew themselves before me...I realized that art in general is much more powerful than I had thought, and that painting could develop the same kind of powers that music possessed." And finally, as he said in his *Rückblicke* (1913), it was the news of the "splitting of the atom" that made him believe that science was destroyed: "Everything became insecure, shaky and soft."

What distinguishes Kandinsky's abstract work produced before the First World War from all earlier attempts of a similar kind is the convincing artistic result. They were, quite evidently, pictures, not experiments. In those years, Kandinsky was realizing his ideas with passionate verve, stimulated by the thought that he was conquering a new world. All his works of that period are the "abstract expressions" of wild animation, explosive in the seething upsurge of the forms, in the dynamic tension of the colors. They closely resemble the works of the *Brücke* artists in their vitality. One can follow step by step the way in which the subject is effaced in these pictures. Certain abbreviated signs appear. The frequently repeated three parallel black lines are an example. They are a rudimentary form of the troika (in bird's-eye view). Certainly, this configuration does not "mean" a troika; it is a paraphrase. There are a number of such fragments that have ended in hieroglyphic form: riders, water, saints, and the cupolas of Moscow. Although these signs as such are unknown to the uninitiated spectator, he senses the import of the message. Kandinsky's early nonobjective pictures possess such a high degree of artistic conviction because the vital experience is still present, no matter how cryptically formulated. It is sensible but not tangible. The gap between the content and the form was, however, to become a battlefield for uncontrolled interpretations. For this intangibility was as attractive as the forbidden fruit. And as the usual instruments of interpretation are no longer sufficient, the critic becomes a poetaster and assumes that the "magic," the "mystic," even the "cosmic," have become the content of the pictures. That is not true. As has already been hinted, it is the representation of certain indefinite phenomena, which by their very nature cannot be depicted with exactness but which can nevertheless be understood by the spectator through a kind of sensitive visual communion.

Kandinsky's early abstract paintings are the climax of his work. He was forty-eight years old at the outbreak of the First World War. After abstract art had been created by the effacement of the subject matter, he approached the resulting questions almost from the opposite point of view. He tried to create a grammar of painting. In his research on the basic principles of color and form he was to be supported by the members of the *Bauhaus*.

In Munich Franz Marc was his most understanding friend, who by good advice and creative assistance, helped to bring about the great change in modern German painting. A native of Munich, Marc first wanted to study philosophy, then theology. After having completed his military service, however, he changed his mind and became a painter like his father. His studies with Hackl and Diez in Munich brought him no satisfaction. An extreme emotional sensitivity and a fear of life aggravated his restlessness and scepticism. This psychological condition provided the right basis for the study of Nietzsche, whose influence can be discerned in all Marc's thought and in his style of writing. His art was not founded on craftsmanship although the vivacious sketches of his youth must be accepted as proofs of a promising talent. He shows early signs of looking beyond mere picture-making. A notable success with an exhibition of naturalistic animal pictures did not prevent him from trying to get away from the "arbitrariness of color." The motive behind his turning away from the "desultory fumbling with light" (as he called it) was the search for a criterion of quality in art which would be quite different from anything taught before. During the war he wrote:

> I saw the visual image as seen through the waterhen's eye as it dives:
> the thousand concentric rings that encircle every little bit of life.
> I saw the blue of the whispering sky that the lake drinks up; I saw
> the waterhen surfacing again rapturously in a distant spot. Do realize,
> my friends, what painting is: the surfacing of the image in another place.

As far as the pictorial effect is concerned, however, in order to overcome the "arbitrariness of color" a form of expression must be sought in which color through its latent magic power would appear as definite and unambiguous as possible. One should mention that these are not objective laws, but subjective truths, the value of which is limited by space and time. Certainly they are truths, the importance of which may be compared to Goethe's theory of color as opposed to Newton's.

In 1910 Franz Marc discovered the *Neue Künstlervereinigung München*. Here were the people of his own mind whom he needed and had been looking for. He became a member. And when Kandinsky left the group, Marc, as has already been said, was among the few that followed him. The almanac had already been planned before this happened; it was to be "the organ of all the new and genuine ideas of our days." Then followed the Blue Rider exhibitions.

Marc loved animals. He had a good friend in his dog "Schlick" and he kept deer in his garden. "The impious people around me (above all the men)," he wrote during the war, "do not arouse my real feelings, while the animal's innocent attitude towards life evokes all that is good in me."

With Franciscan devotion he turned to the animal world. There he recognized the pure creation that fulfilled its destiny in sacrifice. Thus he did not see his animals with the eyes of a stalker; he rather stripped them of the adventitiousness of their natural existence in his paintings and elevated them to the sphere of sacred legends. His pictures are like the celebration of a message full of hope. The solemnity of the colors, the pure concord between the animals' bodies and the surrounding landscapes, and the simple greatness of the lyric atmosphere, create a kind of fairy paradise, in which the animal, transfigured by its participation in the universe, becomes the expression of a religious feeling. Franz Marc painted animals neither as "existences," nor as "symbols." It is the aura of innocence emanating from the animal, the purity and goodness, which is given expression in his pictures. Blue, red, and yellow horses, red deer — in their intrinsic, joyful colorfulness, which nevertheless does not exclude an ominous possibility, they all become artistic revelations of his mystic feeling of oneness with the universe.

Stimulated by his interest in the young European *avant-garde,* and driven by an inner necessity to bring his painting into line with what he conceived of modern natural sciences, Franz Marc underwent a stormy development in the few years that were still granted him. "I could not reconcile modern science with my kind of art. It had to be done, however, and not *au détriment des sciences,* but with absolute respect for European scientific thought. Science is the basis of our European civilization: if we really wish to have an art of our own it cannot live contrary to the discoveries of science."

Though Franz Marc and Kandinsky agreed in their intellectual conception of abstract painting, the paths by which they realized their aims were not the same, and the results also were as different as was to be expected from such diverse temperaments and characters. Line played scarcely any part in Marc's work and there is no hieroglyphic reduction of the motif. Marc thought in terms of areas of color which are full of crystalline refraction and which overlap here and there — in accordance with the superimposed planes. Trees, houses, and cattle, resolutely enclosed within the color structure, disappear into significant signals in the kaleidoscopic sea of color.

In 1914 Marc went to the front with the German army. In 1916 he fell at

Verdun. During one of his leaves he worked over his picture *Tyrol,* which he had painted in 1913, and added the Madonna. This picture, more so than the abstracts, even more than the pages of his frontline sketchbook with its *Magical Moment,* and the *Arsenal for Creation,* represents probably his artistic testament: the world of his beloved mountain landscape, transfigured by the vision of divinity.

Whereas the painting of Franz Marc and Kandinsky sprang from their volition and compulsion, August Macke was more naïve and perhaps more gifted. "Of all of us, he gave color its clearest and purest tone, as clear and pure as his whole being." That was written by Franz Marc of his friend, who had been killed in France in 1914 at the age of twenty-seven. No matter how unnatural Kandinsky's theoretical speculations appeared to his naïve artistic nature, and however sceptical his criticism became of Kandinsky's artistic production, Macke nevertheless found himself at first very much in agreement with the Blue Rider. In 1910 he saw some of Marc's works at Brackl's in Munich, and consequently visited him. A spontaneous, warmhearted friendship developed out of this meeting. Macke had not yet found himself; his studies in Düsseldorf and a few months with Lovis Corinth had borne no fruit. Trips to Paris together with Bernhard Koehler, the great collector and art patron, had widened his horizon and opened his eyes, but he was not yet able to integrate all he had seen. In 1909 he went to Tegernsee for a year with his young family. The exhibition of the *Neue Künstlervereinigung* — especially the pictures of Münter and Jawlensky — helped to indicate the way for him as it did for Marc. But he held himself aloof from the others. "For lack of self-assurance I can never become a great artist." After Kandinsky and his friends had left the group, Macke worked intensively with them on editing the almanac. But only one oil — *Storm* — painted in Marc's attic studio at Sindelsdorf during the preparation of the almanac, gives an artistic expression to the unity of their intellectual efforts.

After his first tentative steps, in which instinctive assurance and critical sense were combined, the decisive experience of his life was his meeting with Delaunay. In October 1912 he went with Marc to see him in Paris. It was like a revelation. For the sensuous Rhinelander, Braque's or Picasso's analytic Cubism was just as alien as Kandinsky's abstractions. The Futurists, with their attempt to represent a chronological sequence in their paintings, certainly exercised their influence on him. Yet in Delaunay, he found that warmly glowing, resplendent color mosaic which was to become the fulfillment of his own efforts. Although he was most convinced by Delaunay's principle of *fenêtres* [windows], because it liberated the "plastic energies of color," one cannot call him a disciple of "Orphism." How different is Macke's world! Quiet ponds, parks, slender women in long, narrow clothes; silent couples, walking together, ethereal and full of dignity. And then the delicate girlish figures of women in front of milliners' shops, who, though interested in the frills of fashion, nevertheless indulge only in dreams of unfulfilled desires. There is a tender atmosphere of expectancy and farewell.

In April 1914 Macke made the momentous trip to Tunisia with Louis Moilliet and Paul Klee, whom he had known since 1911. Within fourteen days he produced about forty watercolors, a brilliant chain of colorful jewels, in which the "sheer joy of nature" as Macke himself said about them was given shape in its purest form. He was twenty-seven years old and a master. The series is like an illuminated festival of color. The precision, the wide range of color, the skill in changing from depth to transparency, are such as would seem to require a long premeditation. And yet these water-colors, despite all their precision, have at the same time all the freshness and spontaneity of works created directly *in situ*. Within the few months still left him before the outbreak of war he had used up the harvest of this journey.

The African journey also proved a turning point in Paul Klee's artistic development. Up till then he had mainly drawn strange lemur-like, spectral figures, similar to Kubin, and delicately drawn landscapes. Since 1898 he had been in Munich, studying with Stuck, among others; previously he had been undecided whether to become a musician or a painter. In 1911 he encountered the Blue Rider painters; in their second (graphic arts) exhibition he showed seventeen works. Then followed the journey to Kairouan. Referring to the "dark powers" of the African sun he noted: "I am going to stop work now. Deep inside myself I know for certain that color has caught me . . . I am a painter."

Paul Klee's work can be compared to a magic microcosm, pregnant with secrets. His nature was as clear as it was tender — friends would say, when he played Mozart it was like a dual revelation — and his quiet meditative strength was always working to create poetically and pictorially new artistic realities from the different worlds of nature and the spirit. These qualities made him one of the most important masters of modern painting. Sincerity and a kind of naïve greatness are the characteristics of his works. These traits may sound somewhat commonplace. His art is self-conscious and expressed in half-statements. Sincere and free from sentiment, his naïveté is not that of a child but the fruit of reflection and wisdom. The poles of his work lie far apart. On the one hand he allows his fantasy to run unchecked to absurdity, and, let it be admitted, to perversity, so that the most reckless artistic acrobatics are performed; on the other hand, his creations are profound meditations on undiscovered and unsuspected worlds, or become, especially in his last works, sinister comments about our tragic and involved existence.

At first he occupied a rather peripheral position in the Blue Rider group, even though he was treated with friendly respect. The African journey, however, did not only transform him into a painter, but the special way in which color — through Macke's influence — now became the autonomous element of his artistic work, involved him directly in the artistic problems of the group. Their work was all too soon interrupted by the First World War. Klee brought his work to maturity alone. *Tapestry of Memories; Full Moon; Villa R.; Movement of Gothic Halls; Waterbirds; Message from an Aerial Spirit;* and *Gardens,* are the titles of the small pictures which he produced until the early twenties. He gives pictorial shape to the nocturnal, the shadowy, and the lunar. The drifting sands of memory and sensuous associations form the spiritual basis of his artistic conception which takes shape in the very act of painting. On the other hand, the picture grows from a first creative urge which need not have an original content or form, but which produces its "content" in the actual process of creation. "This association of idea with object may then perhaps provide the inspiration for this or that addition to the picture, and for accessories which, if the artist is lucky, will fit into some place which is still slightly lacking in form, just as if they had always belonged there" (Klee). Since it has now become clear that there were, in the first decade of this century, two centers of preeminent importance for the development of modern art, Paris and Munich, much stress has been placed on the fact that the Blue Rider group was the cradle of abstract art. It further led to the conclusion that Kandinsky, Marc, and the Blue Rider group were all, more or less, tending to abstract painting. This is not true. On the contrary, it was Kandinsky's view that both languages, the abstract as well as the realistic, were two legitimate possibilities of the *avant-garde* of his generation. It was for that very reason, as has already been pointed out, that the *Douanier* Rousseau was shown side by side with a number of paintings by Delaunay in the first exhibition of the Blue Rider.

Gabriele Münter and Jawlensky were the most powerful representatives of the more realistic artists. Münter painted her landscapes and portraits with a naïve freshness, whereas Jawlensky's pictures have a kind of glowing mysticism. His heads — though in most cases real portraits — possess a visionary quality. Jawlensky and Marianne von Werefkin did not, as a matter of fact, participate in the secession from the *Neue Künstlervereinigung* and neither of them exhibited with the Blue Rider group. But personally and artistically they can, or rather, must be considered as congenial. In a Blue Rider exhibition which was organized by the *Sturm* in 1913 they did, finally, join their friends.

Marianne von Werefkin's *salon* was the social center of the Munich *avantgarde*. She had an admirable brain, spoke several languages perfectly, and was the inspiring muse of Jawlensky. Her diary proves that, very early in the century, she had thought a great deal about the possibilities of an abstract art. As a painter, however, she had abstained from realizing those ideas. She always stuck to a figurative form of expression.

And so did Niestlé, who was the most traditional member of the group. It was perhaps only due to his friendship with Marc that he was asked to show his paintings in the first exhibition. Heinrich Campendonk, who had been introduced to the Blue Rider by Macke, was a close follower of Franz Marc. David Burljuk was a member of the Russian *Fauves* and wrote an article in the almanac about the artistic situation in Russia.

In his attempt to conquer new worlds, Kandinsky had come in contact with Steiner's anthroposophy, and he had also made himself acquainted with other esoteric circles who investigated the supernatural. It was primarily due to this tendency that a man like Kubin was invited to show his drawings with the group. Dreamlike spheres full of fantastic animals, ghosts, and spirits were represented with most skillful draftsmanship. It was "the other side" of this world, to quote the title of a famous novel by Kubin, that was mirrored in his drawings.

As for Schönberg's paintings, Kandinsky himself wrote an essay about them in which he said that they were the subjective expression of an inner necessity. This, however, was the definition which the Blue Rider had found in order to formulate their artistic aims. It was not to be a matter of style. A subjective feeling, sincerely felt, had to be transposed into purely formal values . . .

Alfred Kubin, photographed by Angermann, 1921

Gabriele Münter, photographed by Kandinsky, 1906

A LETTER FROM KANDINSKY*

In a letter written in 1930 to Paul Westheim, Kandinsky gave the following account of the early days in Munich:

You ask me to recall what I remember of the beginnings of the Blue Rider.

Today — after so many years — this is a legitimate request and I gladly comply with it.

Today — after so many years — the spiritual atmosphere of this lovely and, despite everything, most dear city of Munich has radically changed. Schwabing, so noisy and restless then, has fallen silent — not a sound out of the place. A pity for the lovely city of Munich and even more of a pity for Schwabing, that slightly comical, more than slightly eccentric and self-assured place where anyone, man or woman . . ., who was not carrying a palette or a canvas or at the very least a portfolio, was immediately conspicuous, like a "foreigner" in a little country village. Everyone painted, or wrote poetry, made music, or danced. In the attic of every house there were at least two studios in which there was not so much painting going on as there was a great deal of talking, arguing, philosophizing, and hearty drinking (more dependent on the state of people's purses than on their morale). Once a Berliner in Munich asked "What is Schwabing?" "It's the northernmost part of the town," answered a local. "Rubbish," said another, "it's a state of mind." Which was much more to the point.

Schwabing was a spiritual island in the world at large, and in Germany, and usually even within Munich itself.

There I lived for many years. There I painted the first abstract picture. There I nursed my thoughts about "pure" painting, about pure art. I tried to proceed "analytically" in order to discover connecting relationships between the various arts; I dreamt of the "great synthesis" of the future, and I felt compelled to share my thoughts not just with the island around me but also with the people outside. I regarded them as stimulating and essential.

And so my first book, *Über das Geistige in der Kunst*, sprang spontaneously from my hastily scribbled notes *pro domo suo;* I had finished it by 1910 and put it away in a drawer because not a single publisher had the

* in *Das Kunstblatt*, Vol. 14, 1930, p. 57

courage to risk the price of publishing it — pretty trifling, at that. Not even the extremely warm interest of the great Hugo von Tschudi was of any help.

That same period saw the ripening of my desire to put together a book (a kind of almanac), the authors of which would be exclusively artists. I had particularly in mind painters and musicians. The pernicious segregation of one art from another, and of "Art" from popular art, children's art and also from "ethnography," the solid walls erected between manifestations of art which to my mind were so closely related and often identical — to put it briefly, the lack of synthesis — left me no peace. It may seem strange today that for a long time I could find no collaborator, no resources, and simply not enough interest to launch this idea.

Those were the vigorous days of the rise of the many "isms," whose propagators had not yet discovered the feeling for synthesis and whose chief interest lay in waging fervent "civil wars."

Almost on the same day (1911-12) two great movements in painting were born: Cubism and Abstract (= absolute) Painting. At the same time there were Futurism, Dadaism, and the soon to be triumphant Expressionism. Things were really humming!

Atonal music and its then universally booed and scoffed-at master, Arnold Schönberg, were causing no less of a stir than these "isms" in painting.

I got to know Schönberg around that time and immediately found him an enthusiastic supporter of the Blue Rider idea. (At that time we only exchanged letters; we did not meet personally until somewhat later.)

I had already been in touch with some of the future authors. But, so far, there was no indication of being able to embody the Blue Rider idea in a concrete form.

And then Franz Marc arrived from Sindelsdorf.

One talk was enough: we understood one another completely. In this unforgettable man I found an example, very rare at that time (and is it not as rare today?), of an artist who could see far beyond the limits of mere "cliquishness" and who was not outwardly so much as inwardly opposed to all restrictive and inhibiting traditions.

The publication of *Über das Geistige* by R. Piper Verlag [first published in German in 1912; the first English translation, by M. T. H. Sadler, was published under the title *The Art of Spiritual Harmony*, London and Boston, 1914] I owe to Franc Marc; he smoothed the way.

We spent whole days, evenings, and sometimes even half the night discussing what action to take. It was obvious to both of us from the very beginning that we must proceed with complete authority in order to achieve complete freedom for the realization of the embodied idea. Franz Marc brought in a very helpful hand in the person of August Macke, then still a very young man. We asked him to collect the ethnographic material, and also worked on it ourselves. He performed his task brilliantly and was also given the job of writing an essay on masks, which he did equally well.

I took care of the Russians (painters, composers, and theoreticians) and translated their articles.

Marc brought a big selection of works from Berlin — thus establishing the "bridge" [*Brücke*] between the Berlin *Brücke* artists and Munich, where they were so far unknown.

"Work, artist, don't talk," some artists said and rejected our invitation to contribute articles. But that belongs to the chapter of rejection, opposition, and indignation, which we won't go into here.

It was a matter of urgency! Even before the book came out, Franz Marc and I organized the first exhibition of the Blue Rider[1] in the Thannhauser Gallery — on the same principles: not to propagate any one "style" exclusively but simply to juxtapose the most varied manifestations of the new painting on an international basis: ". . . to show, by the variety of forms represented, the manifold ways in which the artist manifests his inner desire," I wrote in the introduction.

The second (and last) exhibition was of graphic art and was held in the new gallery of Hans Goltz. I received a letter from Goltz about two years ago, written shortly before his death, in which he spoke with great enthusiasm of those splendid times.

My neighbor in Schwabing was Paul Klee. At that time he was still "small fry." But I can say with justifiable pride that in his tiny drawings of that period (he was not yet painting) I already sensed the great Klee of the future. One of his drawings can be found in the *Almanach Der Blaue Reiter*.

I must mention, too, Franz Marc's extremely generous patron, Bernhard Koehler, Sr., who died quite recently. Without his helping hand the Blue Rider would have remained just a beautiful Utopia, as would Herwarth Walden's first German *Herbstsalon* and a great deal else besides.

It was my plan for the next volume of the Blue Rider to set art and science side by side — origins, evolutionary processes, end purposes. Today

---

1 The name "Blue Rider" came to us around the coffee table in the summer house at Sindelsdorf; we both loved blue, Marc horses, and I riders. So the name came by itself. And made Maria Marc's fabulous coffee taste even better.

I know even better than I did then what the task of the future is: to trace the many small roots back to the taproot.

But then came the war and swept even these modest plans away with it.

However, what is absolutely necessary — inwardly! — can be postponed but never torn out by the roots.

Kindest regards,

Kandinsky

August Macke, photographed about 1910

Paul Klee, photographed by Paula Stockmar in Munich, about 1916

PLATES AND QUOTATIONS

There are only two ways of accounting for this absurd exhibition: either one supposes that the majority of the members and guests of this association are incurably insane or one assumes that we are dealing here with a bunch of shameless bluffers who, not unaware of the current need for sensationalism, have tried to cash in on the boom. I am personally inclined to take the latter view, despite solemn assurances to the contrary, but out of the goodness of my heart I shall opt for the former.

From a review of the second exhibition of the *Neue Künstler-vereinigung München* in the *Münchner Neueste Nachrichten*, 10 September 1910

1   Wladimir von Bechtejeff, *The Tamer of Horses [Rossebändiger].* About 1912

2 Wladimir von Bechtejeff, *Porte de France, Tunis.* About 1906

Munich 1902–14 — time of my youth, of my hopes, of my first venture in art!

Like so many other Russian artists I had come to Munich to study art. I attended the art school run by Professor Knirr, but the real school for me was my surroundings, the influence of the new *milieu*.

I had only just doffed my officer's uniform and was bewildered by the spirit of winged gaiety, unconstrained openness, and goodwill that I found in Munich's artistic circles.

Artists from many lands were drawn to this city of the muses where everything — nature, art treasures and famous schools, as well as the friendly atmosphere — favored the ripening of artistic talents. One quickly made friends.

We were all united by our devotion to art, our desire to penetrate its secrets, and our determination to discover new means of expression. Every success on the part of one artist was welcomed with joy by his colleagues.

After each hard day's work in studios and art schools the evenings were given over to friendship and conversation. We used to meet in cafés or little restaurants like Kati Kobus's, for example, and sometimes at the home of Jawlensky and Werefkin, where the famous artists of that period — Anna Pavlova, Nijinsky, Eleonora Duse, and others — used to call when they were performing in Munich.

My closest friends were the painters Jawlensky, Erbslöh, and Salzmann, and the dancer Sacharov, who had also originally come to Munich as a painter. Frequent trips abroad took me to France, Spain, Italy, and Tunis and presented me with a wealth of new impressions.

But still my most treasured memories remain those personal relationships.

Moscow, 10 May 1966   W. Bechtejeff

Letter from Bechtejeff to Hans K. Roethel

. . . About a year later (1910) a visitor to my studio suggested that I invite Kandinsky and his associates to have a look at my work. This I was reluctant to do, for various reasons; but after some persuasion, I consented to see Kandinsky and ask him round to my place, if he would only come. As it turned out Kandinsky was glad to come, and when he did come — well, the upshot was, that I was invited to cast my lot with him and his friends. However, this was not the immediate result. The immediate result, as I learned much later, was that, quite innocently and unwittingly, I was indirectly responsible for the breaking up of the New Society of Munich. There had long been discussion among the members, who very soon after the formation of the society divided sharply into two opposing factions, of compromisers, or as we would call them: pussyfooters, and inexorables, or as we would call them: radicals. There is no point in calling over the names of members in the first group, for they would all be unknown to you, and it is indeed astonishing to realize how unknown almost every one of them has become in Europe since that day. Outwardly, when they came to my study in a body, soon after Kandinsky's first visit, all was sweetness and light and harmony amongst them, and an outsider like myself could not suspect that there was anything else. The friction arose out of the fear and distrust felt by the compromisers, the backsliding respectables among the group, of the uncompromising independence and honesty shown by the radicals. The reactionaries feared that the radicals were going too far, and they had lost sympathy for their aims; while the other group were disgusted with the smugness and growing exclusiveness and snobbishness of the backsliders, and were by this time convinced that they were only a thinly disguised lot of not too capable academicians. And that was the situation when I came into the picture. It was simply the violent disagreement between the two factions concerning my worthiness to be admitted to membership that finally precipitated the already inevitable break. I had not put myself forward as a candidate for membership in the society, I did not particularly desire membership, and indeed, the thought of membership in any formally organized group of painters has always been unpleasant to me. But there the one faction was determined not to have me, while the other was quite as determined that I should be admitted — although I rather suspect that their determination was at least to some degree conditioned by the resistance of their opponents, and that I happened to be merely one of those convenient though fundamentally unimportant bones of contention which are so often made the excuse for a decisive squabble and the ultimate showdown; although, to be just, I believe that the separation took place under all the dignified aspects of a gentlemen's disagreement . . .

From a lecture by Albert Bloch, "Kandinsky, Marc, Klee: Criticism and Reminiscence," delivered in 1934 at the Denver Art Museum. A photocopy of the manuscript is in the Städtische Galerie, Munich

3   Albert Bloch, *The Boxing Match.* 1912–13

4   Erma Barrera-Bossi, *Interior with Lamp.* 1909

In view of the wholesale rejection which the *Neue Künstlervereini-gung* has experienced in Munich it is perhaps fitting that a different voice should be raised and a different opinion made known.

Clearly the public feels offended by something here: people expect to find easel painting and become nervous and dubious when they don't find one single painting in the style they are used to. Each picture contains an extra something which robs the spectator of his pure enjoyment but which in every instance constitutes the work's principal value: a completely spiritual and dematerialized emotion which our fathers, the painters of the nineteenth century, never even attempted to capture in their paintings. This bold enterprise, that is, the spiritua-lization of the "matter," is a necessary reaction against Impressionism which began in Pont-Aven with Gauguin and has already taken innu-merable forms since then. What seems so promising about this fresh endeavor being made by the members of the *Neue Künstlervereinigung* is the fact that their pictures — besides being highly spiritualized — postulate extremely valuable examples for the use of space, rhythm, and color . . .

There is something almost amusing about the way in which the Munich public has shrugged off this exhibition. People react as if these paintings were isolated tumors growing in a few sick minds, whereas they are in fact simple and austere first steps in virgin country. Do they not realize that the same spirit of fresh creativity is at work today in every corner of Europe, defiantly self-aware?

Franz Marc, *Zur Ausstellung der "Neuen Künstlervereinigung München" bei Thannhauser,* off-print, Munich, 1910

The newly discovered law of all these modern artists is, however, merely the reestablishment of an old tradition whose origins are to be found in all "barbarian" art: the art of the Egyptians, the Assyrians, the Scythians, etc. The rediscovery of this tradition was the sword which slashed the chains of academic conventionality and set the arts free so that, in color as well as in drawing (form), they could step out of the darkness of slavery into the bright path of spring and freedom. What had been considered to be something merely personal — such as the "clumsiness" of Cézanne or the "frenzy" of van Gogh — turns out to be something much greater: they are revelations of new truths and new ways.

These new principles are inexhaustible sources of eternal beauty. Anyone who has eyes to see can draw from them the hidden meaning of line and color. They call, entice, lure men on! Thus will the bonds definitely be broken that once tied art by all kinds of rules to academicism: construction, anatomy, proportion, perspective, etc. — rules that any dauber could eventually master without difficulty — the cookbook of art!

All our professional and amateur critics should be the first to realize that it is high time the dark curtains were flung back and the window opened upon a finer art!

David Burljuk, "Die 'Wilden' Russlands," *Almanach Der Blaue Reiter*, Munich, 1912, p. 18

5 Wladimir Burljuk, *A Dancer (Spring).* About 1910

6 Heinrich Campendonk, *Girl playing a Shawm.* 1914

Heinrich Campendonk was born on 3 November 1889, in Krefeld. He developed a penchant for art at a very early age and considers himself to be one of those relatively few people who learned their craft from scratch. He spent whole summers painting and drawing from nature in the lush meadowlands of the lower Rhine and even today he likes to repeat such exercises whenever his formal resources threaten to dry up. Campendonk's first teacher was Jan Thorn-Prikker, through whom he became acquainted with the work of Vincent van Gogh and Cézanne, and to whom he also owes his first introduction to Giotto and Fra Angelico. After leaving Thorn-Prikker's studio he began by working on his own in the countryside around Krefeld. Later, when circumstances obliged him to earn his living, he went to Osnabrück as an assistant to a historical painter with whom he worked on the cathedral frescoes, learning in the process a great many things about his craft. After a year Campendonk returned to Krefeld where, in complete solitude, he devoted himself entirely to his work. It was during this period that Campendonk painted the works which Kandinsky and Franz Marc happened to come across. Marc invited him to live in Sindelsdorf in Upper Bavaria, and he moved there in October 1911, devoting his time at first to further studies from nature. As Campendonk himself stresses, the years from 1911 to 1914, spent in the Sindelsdorf circle, from which stemmed the first and most powerful impetus in Germany towards a rebirth of art, were the most marvelous of his entire life. Kandinsky was a constant visitor. August Macke, the other Rhinelander in the group, used to spend weeks on end at Sindelsdorf. An almost overwhelming wealth of inspiration was developed among this group of artists. This was the time of the much-discussed "Blue Rider" manifesto and of the preparation of the first Munich exhibition, which took place in 1911 and in which Campendonk participated.

From the biography of Campendonk (based on information supplied by the artist) in Georg Biermann, *Heinrich Campendonk*, Leipzig, 1921, p. 15

... He realized that his artistic mission lay in representing what he emotionally extracted from nature, that is, in making it visible in a form accessible to other people. His goal is no longer the imitation and reproduction of objective nature but the embodiment of the idea he receives from the contemplation of nature.

This is a new kind of creation and as such it necessitates the invention of a new means of expression that is characteristic of this idea. The search for a way of giving appropriate and consistent expression to his ideas even down to the tiniest details of technique constitutes the leitmotive running through the artist's development. Consequently, the formal aspect comes immediately into the foreground. The subject matter plays an utterly subordinate role, although it is closely related to the idea expressed through it, since after all the artist selects the subject best suited to conveying the idea in its simplest form.

E. von Busse, "Die Kompositionsmittel bei Robert Delaunay," *Almanach Der Blaue Reiter*, Munich, 1912, p. 4

7   Robert Delaunay, *Fenêtre sur la ville.* 1914

8   Alexej von Jawlensky, *The Hunchbacked Man.* 1905

Apples, trees, human faces are for me only suggestions to see something else in them — the life of colour, seized with a lover's passion.

Form a letter by Jawlensky, 1905, quoted in
Clemens Weiler, *Alexej Jawlensky*, Köln 1959, p. 225

The artist expresses only what he has within himself, not what he sees with his eyes.

Note by Jawlensky, quoted in *Das Kunstwerk II*, 1948, p. 52

9   Alexej von Jawlensky, *Landscape near Murnau.* 1909

10   Alexej von Jawlensky, *Seated female Nude*. About 1910

Drawing well does not mean drawing "correctly."

Note by Jawlensky, quoted in *Das Kunstwerk II*, 1948, p. 52

Anyone who can hear silence can also see sound and hear gestures.
I have on many occasions laid particular stress on the fact that we
— Clotilde Sacharov and I — do not dance *to* music nor does the
music accompany our dances, but we actually dance the music itself.

What I mean is that we realize the music in visual form,
expressing through movement what the composer has expressed by
means of musical notes.

From Alexander Sacharov, *Réflections sur la danse et la musique*,
Viau, 1943, p. 13

11   Alexej von Jawlensky, *Portrait of the Dancer Alexander Sacharov.* 1909

12   Alexej von Jawlensky, *Still Life with Fruit.* About 1910

The artist does not create what exists in nature nor even what might exist in nature. Nature serves him only as a key to the organ in his soul, metaphorically speaking.

Note by Jawlensky, quoted in *Das Kunstwerk II*, 1948, p. 52

In 1911 I found a personal form and palette and painted powerful
figure paintings and heads with which I made a name for myself.
I went on working like that until 1914.

Just before the war I suffered a great deal in my spirit on account
of family matters, and then came the war ... In our small flat there
[at Saint-Prex on the Lake of Geneva] I had only one little room
in which to work, with a single window. I tried to go on with my
powerful, strongly coloured paintings but I found I couldn't.
My soul would not allow that kind of sensuous painting, although
there was much beauty in my works.

From a letter by Jawlensky to Father Willibrord Verkade,
Wiesbaden, 12 June 1938

13   Alexej von Jawlensky, *Maturity*. About 1912

14 Alexej von Jawlensky, *Spanish Lady*. 1913

A great work of art is like a great shock.

Note by Jawlensky, quoted in *Das Kunstwerk II*, 1948, p. 51

A work of art is a world of its own, not an imitation of nature.

Note by Jawlensky, quoted in *Das Kunstwerk II*, 1948, p. 51

15   Alexej von Jawlensky, *Meditation*. 1918

16 Alexej von Jawlensky, *Meditation, "The Prayer."* 1922

Many of the "constructivist heads" painted after 1918 bear religious titles. Rightly so. It remains one of the inexplicable miracles of art how and why such aggregations of the simplest shapes, reduced to their most basic geometric form, can so completely open the door to a metaphysical world that an essential part of its secret is revealed. Mondrian proclaimed the same sort of thing and in a similar way — similar, particularly, because he also used this kind of ascetic forms.

Hans Konrad Roethel, catalog of the Jawlensky exhibition, Städtische Galerie, Munich, 1964

I sit at my work. These are my most beautiful hours. I work for myself, for myself alone and for my God. My elbows are very painful then. Often I nearly faint with pain. But my work is my prayer — a passionate prayer uttered in paint. I suffer. I must work a great deal and I do so. God knows how long I shall still be able to hold a brush. Oh God! I work with ecstasy and with tears in my eyes and I go on until darkness falls. Then I am exhausted. I sit there motionless, half-fainting and with terrible pains in my hands.
Oh God! Oh God! I sit there, and the darkness envelops me, and black thoughts creep up on me. And the colours drain from all the walls.
I am alone. The silence hums and I hear my heart tremulously beating.
Alone! Alone!

From a letter by Jawlensky, quoted in Clemens Weiler,
Alexej Jawlensky, Köln 1959, p. 126

52

17   Alexej von Jawlensky, *Meditation on a gold background.* 1936

18   Eugen von Kahler, *The Garden of Love*. About 1910–11

Kahler's delicate, dreamy, serene soul, with a certain pure Hebraic undertone — that unquenchable mystic sadness — was afraid of one thing only, of the "ignoble." And his completely and utterly *aristocratic* soul seemed out of place in our age. It was as if this soul had been sent from Biblical days into our time for some clandestine purpose. And it was as if some blessed hand wished to set it free again.

From Wassily Kandinsky, "Eugen Kahler," *Almanach Der Blaue Reiter*, Munich, 1912, p. 54

As a child I spoke a great deal of German (my maternal grandmother was from the Baltic provinces). The German fairy tales I had heard so often then came alive for me. They were turned into reality by the tall, narrow roofs (they have disappeared now) on the Promenade-platz and Maximiliansplatz, the old quarters of Schwabing; and especially the Au (in Munich) which I discovered by accident one day. The blue tramway passed through the streets like an embodiment of that fairy-tale air that makes breathing so easy and joyous. The yellow mailboxes sang their canary-loud song from every corner. I hailed a poster with the inscription "Kunstmühle" and felt I was in a *Kunst-stadt* (city of art) which for me was the same as a fairy-tale city.[1] The medieval pictures which I painted later on stemmed from these impressions. On somebody's good advice I paid a visit to Rothenburg ob der Tauber . . . The journey was completely unreal. I felt as if a miraculous force were pushing me, against all the laws of nature, farther and farther back into the past . . . Only one painting still exists as a result of that trip. It is *The old Town,* which, however, I painted from memory after my return to Munich . . .

Actually in this painting, too, I was trying to capture a certain hour which always was and always will be the most beautiful hour of the day in Moscow . . . The sun melts the whole of Moscow down to a single speck that like some crazy tuba sets all one's senses and all one's soul vibrating . . . To be able to paint this hour seemed to me to be an artist's most inachievable and greatest joy . . .

Lohengrin, however, seemed to me to be the complete realization of that particular Moscow. The violins, the deep bass notes, and above all the wind instruments, embodied for me at that time all the power of that early evening hour. I saw all my colors in my mind; they were there before my eyes. Wild, almost crazy lines traced themselves before me. I did not dare use the expression that Wagner had painted "my hour" in music . . .

Wassily Kandinsky, *Rückblicke*, Berlin, 1913

[1] Kandinsky is making a pun on the word "Kunstmühle," using it as "art-mill," when the word actually means a "mill using artifical power."

19 Wassily Kandinsky, *Couple on Horseback*. About 1903

20   Wassily Kandinsky, *Gabriele Münter painting in Kallmünz.* 1903

Now about woodcuts. You see, apart from success and sales (which never take first place with me) . . . certain artistic aims and loves are also involved which you don't yet understand because perhaps they haven't come vigorously enough into play yet. Don't try and deter me, though. In this kind of thing I am incorrigibly obstinate and even in the highest degree peculiar. It is quite impossible to have any influence on me at all in this respect. Nor should you try and find out the purpose of this or that piece, for they all have only one purpose – I have to do them, because I cannot free myself of that kind of thought (or perhaps dream) in any other way. Neither do I have any practical application in mind. I just have to do the thing. Later on you'll understand this better. You say it's "play." Absolutely! Everything the artist does is but play. He tortures himself to try and find an expression for his thoughts and feelings, he speaks through color, form, drawing, sound, words, etc. What for? Big question! I'll tell you more about that when I see you. Superficially just play. For him (the artist) the question "What for?" hasn't much meaning. He only knows the question "Why?" That is how works of art are created, and also things that are not yet works of art but stages on the way towards them, things that are nevertheless small glimmering lights singing in the dark. The first and equally the second ones (the first are all too rare) *must* be created because otherwise one has no peace. In Kallmünz you saw the way I work. That's how I do everything that I have to do: it's there within me, ready, and it must find a way of expressing itself. When I play like that I tremble in every nerve, my whole body resounds with music and a god is within my heart. I don't give a damn whether it's hard or easy, whether it takes a long time or comes quickly, nor whether or not it has any practical use. Now and then I come across someone who is grateful to me for my work and who gets something out of it.

. . . I'm very pleased, I really am, that you ask so much of me, but don't expect everything in every piece because for one thing that's hardly possible and — if it were possible — it would be harmful and bad for the work. Best example — Munich art. Right, then the rest when we see each other again.

. . . I will make you strong and vigorous and healthy yet . . . and a god will speak to us both. Bliss, bliss! That inner happiness. The full life. Poetry — the true and genuine poetry . . .

From a letter by Kandinsky to Gabriele Münter, 10 August 1904

55

In practical life you don't often come across a person who wants to go to Berlin and gets off the train at Regensburg. In spiritual and intellectual life it is quite a common thing to get off at Regensburg. In fact, sometimes the train engineer does not want to go on and everybody gets out at Regensburg. How many people, looking for God, come to a halt before a carved wooden figure? How many artists find themselves confined to a style that some other artist, whether it be Giotto, Raphael, Dürer, or van Gogh, had already used for his own purposes?

Wassily Kandinsky, "Über die Formfrage," *Almanach Der Blaue Reiter*, Munich, 1912, p. 78

21   Wassily Kandinsky, *Beach Chairs in Holland*. 1904

22   Wassily Kandinsky, *Portrait of Gabriele Münter*. 1905

But I soon discovered about that time (1901) that every head is a thing of perfect beauty, even if it first appears to be extremely "ugly." It was, as a matter of fact, the natural law of construction, so completely and faultlessly apparent to me in every head, that gave it this touch of perfection. Many times, looking at an "ugly" model, I used to say to myself, "How well done." And, indeed, there is an infinite mastery that manifests itself in every detail: a nostril, for example, always awakens in me the same feeling of admiration as the flight of a wild duck, the junction of leaf and twig, a frog swimming, the pelican's beak, etc., etc.

Wassily Kandinsky, *Rückblicke*, Berlin, 1913

Even as a child I knew those exhilarating hours of inner tension which promise the embodiment of some idea. Those are hours of quivering emotion, of a confused longing that demands the realization of something not yet conceivable, that weighs upon the heart and fills the soul with restlessness by day, and by night it brings on fantastic dreams full of delight and terror. Like so many children and adolescents I tried to write poems, which sooner or later I would tear up. I remember that drawing used to ease this state of mind I tried to describe, that is to say, it allowed me to live outside time and space so that I was also no longer aware of myself.

Wassily Kandinsky, *Rückblicke*, Berlin, 1913

23   Wassily Kandinsky, *Night*. 1906–7

24 Wassily Kandinsky, *Grüngasse, Murnau.* 1909

When I was painting studies from nature I used to let myself go. I did not worry about houses or trees but spread strips and dots of paint on the canvas with a palette knife and let them sing as loudly as I could make them. Resounding within me was the early evening hour in Moscow, and before my eyes I had the powerful, richly colored . . . air and light of Munich.

Wassily Kandinsky, *Rückblicke*, Berlin, 1913

For many years I have searched for a way of letting the viewer "go for a walk" in a painting and of making him lose himself in it. Sometimes I succeeded, too: I could tell from watching him.

Wassily Kandinsky, *Rückblicke*, Berlin, 1913

25   Wassily Kandinsky, *Mountain.* 1909

26　Wassily Kandinsky, *Improvisation 6 [Afrikanisches]*. 1909

The horse carries the rider with strength and swiftness. But it is the rider who guides the horse. A talent will bring an artist with strength and swiftness to great heights. But it is the artist that directs his own talent. I am here referring to the element of "consciousness" or "calculation" in his work, or whatever else you like to call it.

Wassily Kandinsky, *Rückblicke*, Berlin, 1913

Once while in Munich I underwent an unexpectedly bewitching experience in my studio. Twilight was falling; I had just come home with my box of paints under my arm after painting a study from nature. I was still dreamily absorbed in the work I had been doing when, suddenly, my eyes fell upon an indescribably beautiful picture that was saturated with an inner glow. I was startled momentarily, then quickly went up to this enigmatic painting, in which I could see nothing but shapes and colors and the content of which was incomprehensible to me. The answer to the riddle came immediately: it was one of my own paintings leaning on its side against the wall. The next day, by daylight, I tried to recapture the impression the picture had given me the evening before. I succeeded only halfway. Even when looking at the picture sideways I could still make out the subjects; and that fine thin coat of transparent color, created by last night's twilight, was missing. Now I knew for certain that the subject matter was detrimental to my paintings.

A frightening gap of responsibility now opened up before me and an abundance of various questions posed itself. And the most important of them was: what was to replace the missing subject?

Wassily Kandinsky, *Rückblicke,* Berlin, 1913

27   Wassily Kandinsky, *Garden*. 1910

28   Wassily Kandinsky, *Romantic Landscape.* 1911

At some predestined hour the time is ripe for decisions. That is to say, that the creative spirit (which one may call the abstract spirit) finds access first to a single soul, and later on to many, and sets up a yearning therein, an inner urge.

When the necessary conditions for the ripening of a precise form are fulfilled then this longing, this compulsion, gains the power to create new values in the human spirit, values which — consciously or unconsciously — begin to become alive in man.

From this moment on man is constantly trying — consciously or unconsciously — to find a material form for the new values that exist in spiritual form within him.

This is man's search for the materialization of spiritual values. Material is here a kind of stockpile from which the spirit draws what it needs at any given time, just as the cook does from the larder.

Wassily Kandinsky, "Über die Formfrage," *Almanach Der Blaue Reiter*, Munich, 1912, p. 74

And finally the following statement must be made: it matters not whether the form is personal, national, stylistic, whether or not it stands within the contemporary mainstream, whether it is related to a few or to many other forms, or whether it is unique or not, etc., etc.; but the most important point in the question of form is whether or not it springs from inner necessity.[1]

[1] That is, form must never be uniform: works of art are not soldiers. One and the same form can on one occasion be the best thing for a particular artist and on another occasion the worst. In the first case it is rooted in inner necessity, in the second case in external necessity: ambition and greed.

Wassily Kandinsky, "Über die Formfrage," *Almanach Der Blaue Reiter*, Munich, 1912, p. 78

29   Wassily Kandinsky, *Improvisation 19.* 1911

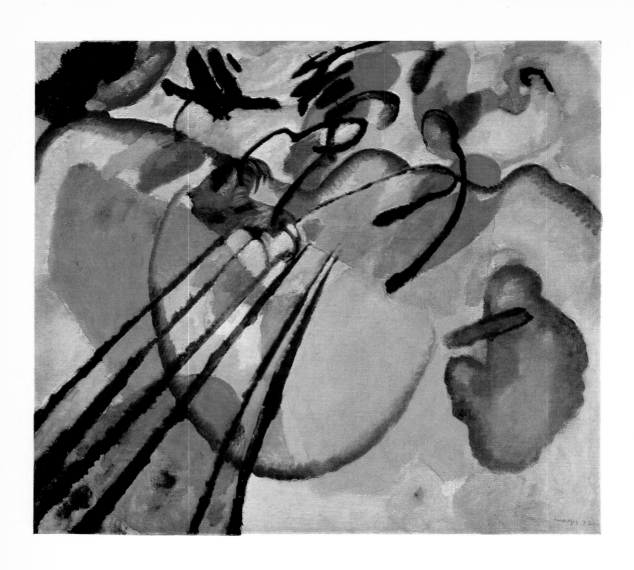

30 Wassily Kandinsky, *Improvisation 26 (Oars)*. 1912

Form is the external expression of inner content.

Consequently no one should make an idol of form. No one should defend a form beyond the period during which it can serve as an expression for the inner voice. And no one should, therefore, seek salvation in *one* form only.

This statement must be correctly understood. The perfect form (that is, medium of expression) for a really creative and not merely an imitative artist is the one that best expresses his mission.

Since form is simply an expression of content and since content differs with different artists, *different forms can exist at the same time and be of equal value.*

Necessity dictates the form. Fish that live at great depths have no eyes. The elephant has a trunk. The chameleon can change its color, etc., etc.

Form, then, reflects the spirit of the individual artist. Form bears the stamp of his *personality*.

Wassily Kandinsky, "Über die Formfrage," *Almanach Der Blaue Reiter,* Munich, 1912, p. 75

Painting is like a violent and thunderous collision between different worlds that are destined to create a new world by fighting each other, the new world being the work of art. Technically every work of art comes into being in the same way as the universe — through catastrophes, which out of the cacophony of all the instruments finally become that symphony we call the music of the spheres. The creation of a work of art is like the creation of a world.

Wassily Kandinsky, *Rückblicke*, Berlin, 1913

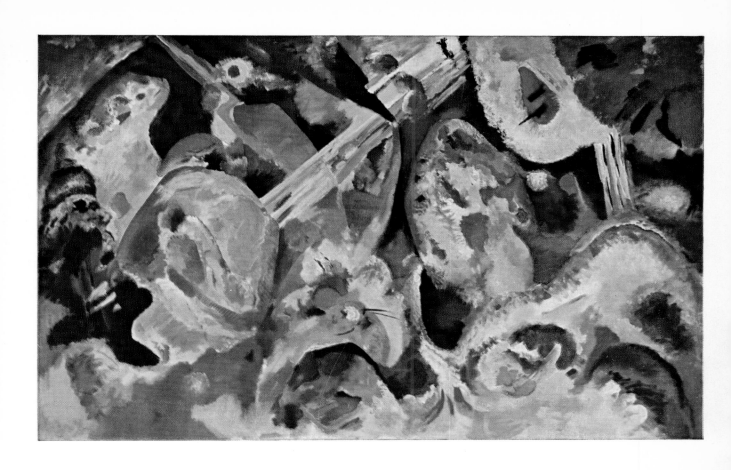

31   Wassily Kandinsky, *Improvisation The Flood.* 1913

32   Wassily Kandinsky, *Horsemen of the Apocalypse II.* 1914

In many ways art resembles religion. The development of the arts does not consist of new discoveries which supersede old truths and dismiss them as aberrations (as is apparently the case with science). Its development lies in sudden illuminations resembling flashes of lightning, in explosions bursting in the sky like fireworks that scatter whole "bouquets" of variously twinkling stars around them. These flashes throw a brilliant light upon new perspectives and new truths which are basically no more than organic developments, the organic increase of earlier wisdoms . . . Would the New Testament have been possible without the Old? Would this age on the threshold of the "third" revelation be thinkable without the second?

Wassily Kandinsky, *Rückblicke*, Berlin, 1913

The communication of what is secret by what is secret:
is not that the content?

Wassily Kandinsky, foreword to the second exhibition of the *Neue
Künstlervereinigung München*, Munich, 1910–11

33　Wassily Kandinsky, *Improvisation Gorge.* 1914

34   Wassily Kandinsky, *Large study for the summer panel for the*
Campbell apartment in New York. 1914

The Art of today . . . does not only reflect the spiritual achievements already acquired but also enshrines, as a materializing force, the spirituality that is ripe to the point of revelation.

The manifestations that the spirit has drawn from the stockpile of "matter" can be divided between two poles.

These two poles are: 1. the great abstraction
                         2. the great realism.

They offer two paths which lead in the end to one and the same goal.

Between these two poles lie many different harmonies combining abstract and realistic elements.

These two elements have always been present in art and used to be referred to as the "purely artistic" and the "objective." The former found expression in the latter and the latter, naturally, lent itself to the former. It was a complex balancing process which apparently sought the culmination of its ideals in a state of perfect equilibrium.

And it seems today as if one no longer sees this ideal as a goal . . .

Wassily Kandinsky, "Über die Formfrage," *Almanach Der Blaue Reiter*, Munich, 1912, p. 82

And so I entered at last the realm of art, which, like nature, science, political life, etc., is a realm unto itself, governed by laws of its own which are applicable to it alone, and which together with all other realms forms, in the final analysis, that great Kingdom which we can only divine.

Today is the great day of one of the revelations of that Kingdom. The interrelations of the individual realms became evident as if illuminated by a flash of lightning; they became, surprisingly, alarmingly and blissfully clear. Never before have they been so strongly bound together; and never before so sharply set apart. This lightning flash is the offspring of the dark sky of the spirit that hung over us, all black, stifling, and dead. It is the beginning of the great age of the spirit, the revelation of the spirit. Father — Son — Spirit.

Wassily Kandinsky, *Rückblicke*, Berlin, 1913

35 Wassily Kandinsky, *Untitled Improvisation*. 1914

36   Paul Klee, *Virgin in a Tree*. 1903

Virgin in a Tree. Technically more advanced through the use of different thicknesses of line. First I drew and etched the lines of the tree. Then I did the modeling of the tree and the contours of the body, and then the modeling of the body and the two birds.

The poetic content is basically the same as *Woman and Animal.* The animals (the two birds) are natural and they form a couple. By her virginity the woman wants to be something special without, however, cutting a very happy figure. Criticism of the bourgeois society.

Note from Klee's diary (no. 514, summer, 1903)

The work in my studio will become a good deal more lively. I have succeeded in transplanting "nature" directly into my style. The term "sketch" is now surpassed. Everything is going to be Klee, whether the gap between impression and creation is a matter of days or only moments.

If ever I cannot express myself "off the cuff," all I shall have to do is go out hunting and shoot as best I can. The production need never be held up then, never again. Naturally a certain dualism will at first be unavoidable. Shall I ever get that far in the realm of color as well? At any rate one more barrier has been broken down, the toughest and most obdurate an artist has to face.

Note from Klee's diary (no. 757, February-March 1906)

37   Paul Klee, *Still Life with Cacti*. About 1906

38 Paul Klee, *Two Statues.* 1908

Oh, the line! My lines of 1906/7 were my own, original and specifically mine. But even so I had to break away from them; some kind of cramping force was threatening them, and even something too ornamental. Briefly, I paused in alarm, even though those lines were deeply felt inside me.

The change was quite abrupt; I devoted the summer of 1907 to studying nature, and used these sketches as a basis for my black and white landscapes on glass of 1907/8.

Hardly have I reached this stage, when nature begins to bore me again. The perspectives are too tedious. Should I now distort them? (I have already tried to do so in a mechanical way.) Or how can I most freely bridge the gap between within and without?

Oh gorgeous line of the arch of that bridge — the day will come!
[O entzückende Linie des Schwunges dieser Brücke — dereinst!]

Note in Klee's diary (no. 831, July-August 1908)

There are some days that are like bloody battles. Now it's the dead of night, but not for me, for the others, for the thick-skinned, who do not feel the battle. They make a bit of music, sing their vulgar little songs, then go to bed.

I can't get to sleep. It's still glowing within me: I can still feel it burning here and there. I go to the window for some cool air and find everything outside lifeless, extinct. Just one little window still alight, very far off. Perhaps there's another person sitting there? Somewhere, surely, I'm not entirely alone! I can hear the notes of an old piano, the moaning of another casualty.

Opportunity to do a lot of oil painting in my new studio (Feilitzschstrasse 3/4). All kinds of experiments, all directed strongly towards tonal values. Now and then a small liberty, like the *Boy in a fur-collared Coat.*

Notes from Klee's diary (no. 833, July-August 1908 and no. 851, January 1909)

39   Paul Klee, *Boy in a fur-collared Coat.* 1909

40   Paul Klee, *Female Dancer.* 1912

Kandinsky, about whom I have spoken before, who lives next door and whom Luli [Louis Moilliet] calls Shlabinsky, keeps on attracting Luli enormously. Luli often goes round to see him, sometimes taking some of my works with him and bringing me back pictures by this Russian which appear to have no subject. Very strange paintings they are.

Kandinsky wants to form a new artists' association. Since meeting him personally I have come to have faith in him. He definitely is somebody, and he has an exceptionally beautiful and clear head.

We first met in a place in the city with Amiet and his wife (who happened to be passing through Munich). In the tram going home we decided to keep in touch. In the winter I joined his "Blue Rider" group

. . . There are, indeed, still primeval examples of art — in ethnographic museums, for example, or at home in one's children's nursery. Reader, laugh not! Children can do it too, and there is wisdom in the fact that they can also do it! The more helpless they are, the more informative their examples, and they too need to be protected against corruption at a very early age. A parallel phenomenon appears in the works of the mentally ill, and here neither "child's play" nor "madness" is an insult that carries any weight. All this needs to be taken very seriously indeed, more seriously than the contents of all our picture galleries, when it comes to the reformation taking place today. If, as I believe, the streams of yesterday's tradition have really run dry, and if those reputedly indefatigable pathfinders (our so-called liberal gentlemen) only appear to look healthy and fresh but are actually, in the light of history, in the last stages of exhaustion, then a great moment has arrived and I hail all those who are working on the reformation now underway.

The boldest among them is Kandinsky, who is trying to exert his influence through writing as well (*Das Geistige in der Kunst*, published by Piper).

Notes from Klee's diary (no. 903, autumn 1911 and no. 905, January 1912)

Nature can allow herself to be lavish in everything; the artist must economize down to the last detail.

Nature is eloquent to the point of confusion; the artist should properly be reticent. In addition, it is essential never to begin a painting with a preconceived idea of what it will look like when finished. Rather, one should devote oneself entirely to that part of the painting one is working on at any given time. The overall impression will then be underpinned by considerations of economy — the effect of the whole will be based on a bare minimum.

Discipline and will are everything. Discipline in regard to the work as a whole, will in regard to the individual parts. Will and ability are very much one thing here: without talent there can, in this case, be no will *[Wer nicht kann, kann hier nicht wollen]* . . .

If my things sometimes give an impression of "primitiveness," it can be explained by my discipline. It's simply economy, to reduce the effect to a minimum; that is to say, it is the highest degree of professionalism. Hence it is the opposite of true primitiveness.

Incidentally, I saw eight paintings by Cézanne in the *Sezession*. He is my teacher *par excellence,* much more so than van Gogh.

Note from Klee's diary (no. 857, May 1909)

41   Paul Klee, *Corner of a Garden.* 1910

42   Paul Klee, *Miraculous Draught of Fishes.* 1913

A good catch of fish is a great comfort.

Note from Klee's diary (no. 183, summer 1901)

Let me take an analogy, if I may, the analogy of the tree. The artist has studied this many-sided world and has, we will suppose, quietly found his way about, more or less. In fact, he knows his way about so well that he is able to articulate the sequence of appearances and experiences. This orientation among the things of nature and life, this sense of order for the most ramified structure, I should like to compare to the roots of a tree. From there the sap rises to the artist and moves through him and through his eye. He occupies the place of the trunk. Moved and driven by the power of the flowing sap, he transforms what he visualizes into his work. In all directions the foliage of the tree unfolds itself silently and visibly in time and space; and so does the artist's work.

From Paul Klee, "Über die moderne Kunst," lecture given at Jena, 1924; published in Berne, 1945, p. 11

Straßen Kreuzung 1913 27,   Klee 1913 27.

43   Paul Klee, *Crossroads*. 1913

44   Paul Klee, *Suburb (Munich North)*. 1913

Last autumn I began to introduce some order into my scratchings. I start with the line, as before; but now I know what to do with the planes in between. Twelve years of inner turmoil have passed. First with blinkers, myself. Then without blinkers, no self. Now without blinkers, myself again. It's a good thing I knew nothing then nor anticipated how long the journey would be.

From a letter from Klee to his friend E., Munich, 18 May 1911

When I mention who Franz Marc is I must confess who I am, because many of the things I participate in belong to him too. He is more humane; he loves more warmly, more explicitly. He treats animals as though they were humans, raising them to his own level. Earthliness is closer to him than *Weltgeist [in Marc steht der Erdgedanke vor dem Weltgedanken]* ...

There was a Faustian element in him, the element of the unredeemed. Eternally questioning, is it true? Possibly even using the word heresy. But none of the quiet confidence of faith. Many times, recently, I feared he might one day become something quite different from the person he is now ...

Characteristic of him was a feminine urge to share the richness of his heart with everybody. The fact that not everybody followed him filled him with doubts about the path he was taking. I often was afraid that, after the fermentation, he might fall into a kind of earthly simplicity ...

My ardor is more that of the dead or that of the unborn. No wonder that he found more love. His noble sensuality attracted many by its warmth. Marc was still one of a species, not a cosmic man. I remember his smiling at me when earthly moments passed me by.

Art is like creation and holds good for now and forever. My work probably lacks a general philanthropy. I do not love animals or other living creatures with temporal wholeheartedness. I neither look down on them nor raise them up to my level ... My love is remote and of a religious nature. Everything "Faustian" is alien to me ... A thousand questions remain unasked, as if solved. There are neither doctrines nor heresies. The possibilities are too endless, only faith in them lives within me in a creative way.

Do I radiate warmth? Coolness? Beyond the point of white heat there is no question of either. And because not many reach that point, few are affected. No sensuality, be it ever so noble, can bridge the gap to the many. Man in my work is not one of a species but a kind of cosmic element. My earthly eye is too farsighted and usually overlooks the most beautiful things. Hence it is often said of me: "But he doesn't see the most beautiful things."

Art is an image of creation. God did not particularly bother with the incidental accidents of creation, either.

Note from Klee's diary (no. 1008, summer, 1916)

45   Paul Klee, *South wind [Föhn] in Marc's Garden.* 1915

46   Paul Klee, *Town R.* 1919

No one would expect the tree to grow its branches identically to its roots. Everybody understands that there can be no exact mirror-relationship between above and below . . . Obviously because of the different functions there must be clear-cut differences.

But the artist, for whom such differences are a creative necessity, is the very person who is sometimes criticized for making them. Some people have even gone so far in their zeal as to accuse him of impotence and deliberate falsification.

Yet all he does is to gather up and pass on that which rises out of the depths. He neither serves nor commands; he simply mediates.

The position he occupies is thus a truly modest one. And the beauty of the tree's crown is not that of the artist himself; it has merely passed through him.

From Paul Klee, "Über die moderne Kunst," lecture given at Jena, 1924; published in Berne, 1945, p. 13

Am I God? I have so many great things stored up within me! My head is burning and fit to burst. My mind must have an overabundance of strength.

More to the point: genius sits in a glasshouse — an unbreakable one giving birth to ideas. After each birth it falls into madness. Through the window it grabs the next person passing by. The demon's claw slashes, the iron fist pounds *[Die Dämonskralle hackt, die eiserne Faust packt]*. You used to be my model, it sneers between rows of jagged teeth, now you're material for my work. I'm going to fling you at the wall of glass so that you stick there like paste . . . (Then the art lovers come along and look at the gory work from outside. The photographers arrive. "New Art," it says the next day in the papers. And the art magazines give it a name that ends in -ism.)

Note from Klee's diary (no. 690, August 1905)

47   Paul Klee, *The Wild Man.* 1922

48　Paul Klee, *Archangel*. 1938

In this world I am totally incomprehensible. I dwell just as much with the dead as with the unborn. Rather closer to the heart of creation than is usual. And nothing like close enough.

Do I radiate warmth? Coolness? Beyond the point of white heat no such question can be raised. When I am most removed I am most devout. Here sometimes I can be mischievous . . . The priests are just not devout enough to see it, and the scribes are just a bit annoyed.

Note by Klee for Leopold Zahn's book, *Paul Klee — Leben, Werk, Geist*, Potsdam, 1920

A kind of delirium took hold of me. During the next six months, driven on by my pain, I produced the best things I had ever done. I anesthetized myself with work. My drawings, bound to the gloomy and pale moods of the Dreamland, were concealed expressions of my misery. I made a thorough study of the poetry of dank courtyards, hidden attics, shady back rooms, dusty flights of winding stairs, gardens run wild and overgrown with nettles, the pale colors of tiles and parquet flooring, dark smokestacks and the curious community of chimneys. I produced variation after variation on the one basic note of melancholy, the wretchedness of loneliness and the struggle with the incomprehensible world. Apart from these numerous works which I did for the public and which I tried to get published in the *Traumspiegel** I produced other things as well. I did several small series of works intended only for the few. In these I tried to create completely new formal structures according to secret rhythms of which I had become aware; they writhed about, bunched up and exploded against one another. I went even further. I renounced everything except line, and during these months I developed a curious linear system. It was a fragmentary style, more written than drawn, which like a sensitive meteorological instrument recorded every slightest variation in my mood. I called these drawings "psychographics" and wanted later on to write explanations for them. In the field of creative work I found the relief I so much needed. But I was far from being at peace with fate, and fundamentally it was a hybrid life I led.

* In Kubin's book *Die andere Seite,* "*Traumspiegel*" [Dream Mirror] is the newspaper in Dreamland.

Alfred Kubin, *Die andere Seite,* Munich, 1962, p. 98. This famous novel by Kubin, first published in 1909, has recently been translated into English (*The Other Side,* Crown Publishers Inc., New York, 1967).

49   Alfred Kubin, *Thunderstorm*. 1906

50   Alfred Kubin, *In the Jungle*. About 1913

A prime example of such seers of doom is Alfred Kubin. One is drawn by an indomitable force into the terrifying atmosphere of harsh emptiness. This force emanates as much from Kubin's drawings as from his novel *The Other Side*.

Wassily Kandinsky, *Über das Geistige in der Kunst*, Munich, 1912, p. 27

About the same time Franz Marc, founder with Kandinsky of the
"Blue Rider" (a small group of artists to which I also belonged),
suggested the attractive idea of editing a *de luxe* edition of the Bible.
I immediately joined in and took charge of the prophet Daniel.
I visited Marc at Sindelsdorf — spending two wonderful days of sun
and friendship — and all in all, good and promising times seemed to
have come for modern art. Sometimes it was quite alarming to observe
the spirit of bold and ardent resolution that had got hold not only
of many young people but also of quite a few of the older generation.
But I was delighted to witness this process of creative demolition and
reconstruction and to be able, on my frequent visits to Munich, to
experience it and to see for myself, on each occasion, new achievements. Intelligent writers were drawing formal parallels between
works of a thousand years old and those of the present day, and con-
versely exposing contradictions where I could see none at all . . .
Although I had anticipated this whole development, which paralleled
other phenomena of our time, I was surprised, all the same, at the
speed at which it was moving. It was like a brotherhood of all young
artists of Europe; nationality no longer mattered. The art dealers,
sceptical and impervious at first, gradually accepted the new art since
collectors and directors began to sponsor it.

Alfred Kubin, *Dämonen und Nachtgesichte*, Munich, 1959, pp. 46–7

86

51   Alfred Kubin, *The enchanted Prince.* 1923

52　August Macke, *Fishermen on the Rhine.* 1907

In the afternoon I met August Macke at Wildemann's. With that natural, cheerful geniality of his, in which the ideas follow easily and spontaneously upon one another, he told me about his experiences in Berlin and Hamburg, about books he had read, and people he had met. His agile imagination, his generous sense of humor with its delicate feeling for the typical, his naturalness, his knowledge of human nature, based on an unparalleled capacity for appreciating and enjoying life, his lucidity, to which nothing human seems beyond comprehension — all these qualities make him a brilliant *raconteur*. Whether he is talking about people or books or paintings, he is unvaryingly perceptive, and hence always has something original to say. His genius as a painter is beyond all doubt. He is incredibly productive, full of a multitude of conceptions, sharply observant, a consummate sketcher who can create a whole life with a few strokes, and a man who is continually changing, who is learning all the possibilities of painting, and who as a result has naturally acquired a great capacity for penetrating the minds of other artists and their manner of production. He is as much at home with the art of Rembrandt and Leonardo as with that of Monet, and knows in each case the motives underlying that art, principally through his extremely penetrating intuition.

All his paintings are a search for and an education of himself, a striving after knowledge of the most profound kind. To begin with he only experiments, not producing any finished work but often painting two or three pictures in one day, and his sketchbooks already number into infinity. He lives in a condition of constant, fierce self-criticism and so is continually reshaping himself. Nor are his talents in any way confined to painting, for he has excellent taste in literature, both clear and assured, and also takes a certain interest in philosophy and the natural sciences. Musically he is quite unusually receptive, and his acute sense of psychology, though often one-sided, is invariably intelligent, and there are few men with whom I more enjoy talking about people. There is nothing of the transcendental in his nature and all ideas of the beyond are alien to him. Possibly his genius is much too strongly rooted in life. He considers philosophizing on metaphysical problems as a waste of time. He also lacks a historical sense; he sees the present only, and takes life as it comes rather than as it has become. His feelings are profound and elemental. He has, I should say, those frequent moments of ecstasy and undergoes those oscillations of mood between happiness and the most crushing despair that are the prerogative of the great artist, who must know the whole gamut of emotions from his own experience. He is clever enough not to belittle the lofty things he laughs at and caricatures. With the rigor of an Aristophanes he senses the ridiculous in the most beautiful and the most harassing of situations, like, for example, the one he told me about, even when he is himself most deeply involved. His curiosity is insatiable, and he has the capacity to satisfy it. Linked to this is an almost brazen good fortune such as is enjoyed only by those whom the gods favor. His strong sympathies and antipathies never prevent him from reaching an objective judgment, but he needs space and does not lightly do anything that opposes his own individual development or stands in contradiction to his current inclinations. In this regard he is capable of the most ruthless inconsideration. Yet at the same time he has a great capacity for adapting himself to circumstances, and I can hardly imagine any situation that would find him at a loss. He has an aversion to everything soft and feeble, for in all his feelings there reigns a certain greatness. He is one of those sovereign natures, and the most gifted person I know.

Lothar Erdman, diary entry of 30 March 1908

... What a wonderful and enigmatic thing love is. It's the only
thing I bow to ...

From a letter from August Macke to his future wife, Düsseldorf,
17 January 1905

... Oh, if only I could walk with you through the fields and show
you everything. But your letter radiates the same kind of happiness,
the yearning after beauty. You say it all so beautifully and so patently
that I wish I could paint it so clearly. Come, let us be calm, as calm
as this quiet spring evening where just a touch of gold is shining
between the blossoms and where the blossoms glow with a secret light.
So ought our eyes to be. Yes, our eyes are our soul. When we see like
this we are calm. And thank God I see many things that way. Is there
a purer kind of happiness imaginable? The beautiful things we have
discovered ... I look every day at the Japanese blossoming twig,
the grey one next to the woodcuts. It is wonderful, such a reverent
work ... Strange, I am so calm now, so quiet inside, I see so much
beauty ...

From a letter from August Macke to his future wife, Kandern,
16 May 1907

88

53   August Macke, *Portrait with Apples.* 1909

54   August Macke, *A Corner of the Living Room in Tegernsee.* 1910

At the moment I find all my happiness in pure color. Last week I tried to put some colors together without thinking of particular objects like figures or trees . . . The miracle that makes music so mysteriously beautiful works its magic in painting too. Only it needs tremendous vision to coordinate colors like musical notes. Colors have their counterpoint, their treble and bass clefs, their major and minor keys, just as music does. With infinitely fine intuition rather than "knowledge" one would be able to put them in their proper sequence. I have tried it, of course with dubious results, but in doing so the whole principle of Impressionism became clear to me.

From a letter from August Macke to his future wife, 14 July 1907

. . . I don't know whether I deserve to be granted so much happiness
and beauty. But I rejoice, I really rejoice that there are a few people
who regard youth with unprejudiced eyes. One sometimes feels
hampered by Philistines who are generally older than oneself and who
are always on hand with a lot of sober advice which no young person
listens to anyway. Thank you very much for giving me these happy,
carefree days. They mean as much to me as perhaps a couple of years'
work. I see everything quite differently, everything has a kind of
elevation such as I have never experienced before. I usually spend my
lunchtime sitting in one of the large squares watching the fountains
glittering so beautifully in the sun. Paris is full of fountains and I have
grown very fond of them. They are like life itself. They sparkle and
glisten; they're alive! They have no idea why they fly up towards
the sun. People here don't know why they're living either, but they
live. And there are many people who ask far too many questions
about it. They are the sort who never learn, and they die as stupid
as they were before they were born. Here in Paris all the people who
think too much seem to me to be poor devils. There's a dancer here
in one of the theaters, a thoroughbred, a real human being, she dances
like the water in the sunlight and she doesn't know why. And if I
have any talent, which is by no means certain as yet, I want to paint
in such a way that my brush dances just like that across the canvas
— no brown-sauce painting for me. And while doing so, I'll think of
Paris. And you're to blame for the fact that this life here is setting me
free . . .

From a letter from August Macke to Bernhard Koehler, Paris,
18 June 1907

90

55   August Macke, *Portrait of Bernhard Koehler, Sr.* 1910

56 August Macke, *Flowers on the Windowsill.* 1910

All our windows here look out onto a magnificent landscape which we can see day in and day out. We see the pine trees, tall and over-grown with lichen. The mountains, the lake, and the buds waiting beneath their burden of snow for spring to come. And then there's the cat. And dogs and horses and people. This continuous intimacy gives one a tremendous feeling of admiration for nature and everything in it; one feels a part of it and not a stranger who only knows nature from books. All those mountains, those sunbeams, and those animals flow through one's blood like an electric current. For me this is the greatest happiness. The only irritation is the artist's inability to paint it all. But after all, it is only an image that he has to make, a song about beauty.

From a letter from August Macke to Sofie Gerhardt, Tegernsee, 10 February 1910

A sunny day, a cloudy day, a Persian spear, a holy vessel, a heathen idol and a wreath of everlasting flowers, a Gothic church and a Chinese junk, the prow of a pirate ship, the word "pirate" and the word "holy," darkness, night, spring, cymbals and their clashing sound and the guns of dreadnoughts firing, the Sphinx in Egypt and the beauty spot on the Parisian *cocotte's* little round cheek.

Lamplight in Ibsen and Maeterlink, paintings of village streets and of ruins, mystery plays in the Middle Ages and the scaring of children, a landscape by van Gogh and a still life by Cézanne, the propeller's hum and the neighing of horses, the yells of a cavalry charge and the Red Indians' war paint, the cello and the bell, the locomotive's shrill whistle and the cathedral-like character of beech woods, masks and decorations in the Japanese and Greek theaters, and the Indian fakir's mysterious, hollow drumming.

Is not life more than food, and the body more than clothing?

Ideas that appear to be inconceivable express themselves in concrete forms. They become perceptible through our senses as a star, as thunder, as a flower — in other words, as form.

To us form is a secret because it is the expression of hidden force. It is through form that we surmise the secret force, the "Invisible God."

The senses are for us like bridges between the Inconceivable and the Concrete. Contemplating plants and animals is like sensing their secrets.

To hear thunder is to feel aware of its secret. Understanding the language of form is to get closer to comprehending its secret — that is, getting closer to Life.

To create forms is to live. Are not children creators, drawing as they do directly from their emotions, more so than the artist who imitates Greek form? Are not primitive people also artists because they have their own original form which is as powerful as that of thunder?

Thunder expresses itself; flowers, all forces express themselves as form. Including man. He too is driven on by some power to find words for his concepts, to make clear what is obscure and make conscious what is unconscious. This is his life, his task.

As man changes, so his form changes too. The relationship between the many existing forms enables us to distinguish the individual form. Blue becomes "visible" only through red, the bigness of a tree through the smallness of a butterfly, the child's youth through the senility of the aged. One and two make three. The shapeless, the infinite, the void, these remain intangible. God remains intangible.

Man expresses his life in form. Art is an expression of his inner life. The external form is identical with the inner spirit.

Every true form stems from a vital relationship between man and the material forms of nature and art. The flower's scent, the joyful leaping about of a dog or of a dancer, the wearing of jewelry, a temple, a painting, the style, the life of a people, of an epoch.

The flower opens with the dawning of day. The panther crouches at the sight of his prey, and consequently his muscle tension increases. And this bracing of his strength results in the length of his spring. Form and style stem from such a bracing.

August Macke, "Die Masken" [Masks], *Almanach Der Blaue Reiter*, Munich, 1912, p. 21

57 August Macke, *Farmboy from Tegernsee*. 1910

58 August Macke, *Mounted Red Indians.* 1911

Dear Mr. Kandinsky,
Your last letter sounded like the ringing of the *Kaiserglocken*[1] in the
Cologne Cathedral — long and breathtaking. So much good news
gave me great pleasure and I have reread it many times and felt it all
with you. Meantime I was in Berlin and saw many good things.
I particularly liked a certain feeling for style in Heckel and Kirchner.
As to the response to the "Blue Rider," the news is very good indeed.
There was a tremendous lot going on again, and your book was selling,
too (eight copies, I think). The more often I see the exhibition the more
I enjoy the Rousseau and your big painting (with yellow spots) that
impresses me like a fanfare of trumpets. In Berlin . . . I liked Burljuk's
head with the spots. And many other things, including my little Red
Indians, for example.

From a letter from August Macke to Kandinsky, written probably in
January 1912

[1] *Kaiserglocken* were Imperial bells that could be rung only in the
presence of a monarch.

. . . I'm working like mad at the moment. Working really means to
me being totally immersed in enjoying nature, sunshine, trees, shrubs,
people, animals, flowers and pots and pans, tables, chairs, mountains.
I muse about the friendly nodding of the snowdrop, about the rhythm
of branches full of little birds swaying in the sun, about the marvelous
pouncing and prowling of our cat, about the chubby laughter of red-
cheeked apples . . .

From a letter from August Macke to Hans Thuar, 7 March 1910

94

59   August Macke, *The Zoo I.* 1912

60   August Macke, *Carpet of Flowers.* 1913

The vitality of a painted surface derives from the simultaneous sound of red and blue, of lines, curves, etc. The way an artist makes the reds predominate in a picture and by contrast deepens the blues, and the way he organizes the whole tension of the canvas is precisely that kind of mathematics which cannot be expressed in words.

Undated note by August Macke

We are moved by the tensility existing between things in nature. We react to this by trying to give form to it. Life is indivisible. The life of a painting is indivisible. The life of the painting is the simultaneous tension existing between its various parts.

The more the vitality of the tension is reduced the more homogenous the parts or groups of parts within the whole become. The dripping or gushing of a tap. A primed canvas.

The more the vitality of the tension grows the less homogeneous the shapes and patterns in a work of art become. A sonata by Mozart — a still life by Renoir or Cézanne.

A characteristic feature of the "new painting" is that one can find these contrasting patterns all over the canvas, whether in color — a clash of red-green-yellow — or in formal conflicts between planes and edges. It seems to me that the clash of contrasting patterns is the basic element of composition of most modern paintings, as opposed to the quiet merging of groups of less violent contrasts in earlier works.

I think the one thing that all "modern" painters have in common — in spite of their individual differences — is the intention to enhance the life of their paintings by making use of such contrasts. Picasso, for instance, parted with his early style, which still possessed the calm of the old masters, and is now out for a vital tension, which he achieves by using a limited number of colored planes. The movement in his paintings results from the clash of juxtaposed planes. Matisse, on the other hand, has developed further the methods of the Impressionists in his own way and has thereby achieved a free expression of the impressions which he receives from nature. He does not always succeed, however, in giving his colors a two-dimensional quality and depth. Delaunay works completely without chiaroscuro and joins or rather separates the contrasting groups of colors in order to create a harmony with intense movement, a forward and backward movement that he uses in his realistic paintings as well as in those works where movement as such is the subject of the painting.

August Macke, "Das neue Programm," essay in *Kampf um die Kunst: Antwort auf den Protest deutscher Künstler*, Munich, 1911, p. 80

61 August Macke, *Promenade.* 1913

62   August Macke, *Our Street in Grey.* 1913

... The new thing I have discovered in painting is this: there are some color harmonies — a certain red and green, if you like — that begin to move and vibrate when you look at them. If you are looking at a tree in a landscape you can look either at the tree or at the landscape but not at both at the same time because of the stereoscopic effect. To discover the depth-creating energies of color instead of resting content with a dead chiaroscuro is the finest goal we can set ourselves.

From a letter from August Macke to Hans Thuar, Hilterfingen, 12 February 1914

A work of art is a parable, it is man's thought, an autonomous idea of an artist, a song about the beauty of things; a work of art is the noble, differentiated expression of man who is capable of something more than merely saying: "Isn't that beautiful!"

Undated note by August Macke

63   August Macke, *A Millinery Shop.* 1913

64   August Macke, *Promenade on a Bridge.* 1913

If the warning cries of the passive crowd counted for anything in art this planet would probably never have grown a single Gothic church much less an orchid.

Undated note by August Macke

I am becoming more and more aware of the wonderful possibilities that art can offer. I'm also much clearer now about so-called abstract painting. I recognize its importance (without, however, attributing importance to it alone!) quite clearly, as clearly as two and two make four.

It has become particularly clear to me recently that it is not space (plane) alone that is effective in a painting but that plane and time are inseparable. This is very important when looking at a painting. It becomes obvious when the painting is very large and is hung in a long, narrow passage so that one has to walk slowly past it. Looking at a painting like that is like walking past a fence and seeing the individual pales flicker. The trick of the painting, however, consists in the organization of the different lines, spots, colors, human forms, flesh, foliage, nimbuses, frames, columns, arches, domes, roofs.

The wonderful thing about a cathedral or a statue or a painting is the rhythm. A fence is boring; it is as uniform as a heap of sand, as a whitewashed wall, as a nothingness, it is like 1: 1: 1: 1. Vitality is a very bracing force, whether it be the fall from joy to sadness in life, whether it be the slow, steady dawning of a spring day with all its slowly unfolding power, or whether it be the anger that is aroused in a strong person.

A work of art is an image of nature, not a copy. (For if it were a copy we should have to be God himself and create real trees and flesh and blood figures.) What we are inside — our ego — we have to re-create within us continually. The life of our ego is the spark that lights the fuse. The fire that burns down but is always on the lookout for fresh fuel — this fire is our ego. But after the fire the important thing is the ashes. The ashes of the Egyptians, the pyramids and the Sphinx, the ashes of the Gothic age, the ashes of Christ, Napoleon, Frederick the Great. But woe betide those who lose themselves in the ashes, who turn back. The ashes only direct the spark which way to go on burning. It is from the threads that reach us out of the kaleido-scope of history that we know which way to go on.

. . . Nature has to be re-created within us, we experience it afresh from our childhood. The work of art is the result of our experience, of our amazement at the measure of things. The rhythmic element in a work of art is an image of the rhythmic element in nature itself.

From a letter from August Macke to Bernhard Koehler, Bonn, 30 March 1913

100

65   August Macke, *Children with a Goat.* 1913

66 August Macke, *Turkish Café II*. 1914 ·

Anyone who in these last eventful years cared about the new German art or sensed anything of our artistic future knew August Macke. And we, his friends, who worked with him, knew about the unveiled future of this genius. With his death one of the most beautiful and most daring momentums in German art has been abruptly broken off; none of us is capable of continuing it. Each of us moves in his own orbit, and wherever we meet he will always be missing. As painters we know full well that there will be no more of his harmonies; German art must fade by several degrees and will henceforth have a more obtuse and dryer sound. It was he who produced lighter and brighter colors than any of us, as light and bright as he was himself.

The German public of today cannot suspect how much it already owes to this young painter; it cannot know the quantity of his work nor the quality he achieved. Everything he touched and everyone he met came to life, every kind of material and especially the people he drew magically into his spell. How much we painters owe to him! The seed he scattered will yet bear fruit and we, his friends, shall take care that it does not remain concealed.

But his work is cut off, wretchedly and irrevocably. The greedy war is richer by a hero's death, but German art is the poorer by a hero.

Franz Marc, obituary for August Macke

Her maiden name was Maurice and she was from Alsace-Lorraine, but following the early death of her mother she was brought up in a boarding school in the French part of Switzerland, according to strict Calvinist principles of faith and morality. Her rather strong-boned face and figure did not prevent her from being a beautiful woman. In later life she grew into that kind of elderly beauty which people of strong character so often develop, age alone being capable of bringing the severity of such natures to full and harmonious maturity. As a mother she could be strict and severe towards herself and others. She was one of those people who regard art with a certain caution if not suspicion. Even clothed she would only rarely be persuaded to sit for her husband. Because of her genuinely Christian socialism she would not make any distinction between the moralities of upper and lower classes or sanction a so-called free way of life even for the artist. Her moral standards probably even influenced her husband's art, because certain "Makart" tendencies in some of his earlier paintings completely disappeared after his marriage. Though not actually rejecting the aristocratic milieu in which her husband had moved almost exclusively up to that time she nevertheless felt a stranger to it, so that the young man felt compelled to gradually withdraw from such circles . . . The social life of the Marc family was confined to a few intellectual friends . . .

From Alois J. Schardt, *Franz Marc*, Berlin, 1936, p. 10

67   Franz Marc, *Portrait of the Artist's Mother*. 1902

68   Franz Marc, *Jumping Dog (Schlick).* 1904

From now on we have to learn not to look at animals and plants in relation to ourselves but to represent in art our relationship to them . . . Everything in the world has its form, its formula, which we did not invent or discover by laying our clumsy hands on it, but it is something we must grasp intuitively as artists. The result will always be patchy so long as we are confined to this earthbound existence — but do we not all believe in metamorphosis? Why do all artists pursue this everlasting search for metamorphic forms and for the essence of what really lies behind the outward appearance of things?

Franz Marc, *Briefe, Aufzeichnungen und Aphorismen*, Vol. 1, Berlin, 1920, p. 123

. . . Franz Marc was just over twenty when he produced these drawings. They resemble those early morning dreams which, still heavy with night, have already begun to tremble slightly in response to the call of bright day. This gentle half-sleep of earliest youth, which is more like a condition of open-eyed torpidity, a state of paralysis combined with the highest degree of excitement, often has the longest hold over just such very powerful artists. Like the sleeper who is already well aware that he is only dreaming and of whom one can indeed no longer really say he is dreaming, having been for a long time wide awake deep inside but unable to remove the thin veil still covering his eyes, his inert body still being in the grip of sleep though his soul has long been free — so this artist's hand was still tied for a while to habit, custom, and memory, even when his spirit was already wandering far. The young German painter in particular often has this, his inner yearning tending to announce itself at first merely as a vague surging. On top of this surging wave all kinds of things are swimming about pell-mell, some his, some belonging to others, but he fishes around and at first in his great joy does not even ask what he is going to catch. Some masters return to this state in advanced age; they gently doze off again but keep on fishing away as if they were still awake, the hand staying active automatically even after it has ceased to catch anything. Between these two periods — of not yet being awake and of having dozed off again — lies that brief spell of conscious creative work dominated by the artist's will. But perhaps these dark ages of the artist's youth and old age contain more of his true being than is manifest in the bright daylight of his mastership. Mastery, after all, invariably implies self-discipline, and hence narrowing down, even impoverishment, insofar as all our gains must sooner or later be paid for in losses. A man becomes a master by concentrating entirely upon his creative center; the process always involves a kind of retreat from the plenty with which the youth once presumptuously started out and of which only the old man, his hand loosened by time, lets us catch a further occasional glimpse . . .

He lived on an alp with sheep and cows and a couple of good books. At that time some of these paintings were done as little marginal notes, murmured, so to speak, in an undertone while his overflowing soul meditated in deep solitude . . . Thus would St. Francis cut himself a flute and play his thanks to heaven: not much was heard of it, but he felt the better for it. It is St. Francis whom [Marc] resembled in more ways than in just the compassionate intensity of his love for animals. But to us, knowing as we do the freedom, determination, and clarity of will which the young artist achieved, these drawings are a treasured legacy of those blessed hours . . .

Hermann Bahr, *Stella Peregrina*, Munich, 1917

69   Franz Marc, *Orpheus and the Animals*. 1908

70   Franz Marc, *Two Horses*. 1908–9

I am trying to enhance my sensitiveness for the organic rhythm that I feel is in all things, and I am trying to feel pantheistically the rapture of the flow of "blood" in nature, in the trees, in the animals, in the air .... I can see no more successful way towards an "animalization" of art, as I like to call it, than the painting of animals. That's why I've taken it up ...

From a letter from Franz Marc to Reinhard Piper, December 1908

Religions die slowly.

"Style," however, that inalienable asset of the old days, suffered a catastrophic collapse in the middle of the nineteenth century. Since then there has been nothing like style; it has perished the whole world over, as if wiped out by an epidemic. All serious art since has been the work of individuals.[1] Such works have nothing to do with "style," being utterly unrelated to any taste or needs of the masses and having, moreover, been created in spite of their time. They are rebellious fiery signs of a new era . . .

[1] In France, for example, from Cézanne and Gauguin to Picasso; in Germany, from Marées and Hodler to Kandinsky. This is not to imply any kind of evaluation of artists cited but simply to suggest the development of painting in France and Germany.

Franz Marc, "Zwei Bilder," *Almanach Der Blaue Reiter*, Munich, 1912, p. 9

71 Franz Marc, *Deer at Twilight*. 1909

72   Franz Marc, *Young Oak Tree.* 1909

Since nothing happens by chance and without organic reason — not even the loss of style in the mid-nineteenth century — we must assume that today we have reached a turning point of an epoch, similar to the one of fifteen hundred years ago when there was also such a period of transition with neither art nor religion, a period in which the great and ancient passed away and were replaced by the new and unforeseeable . . . And we are convinced that we are able already to annunciate the first signs of the new era.

Franz Marc, "Zwei Bilder," *Almanach Der Blaue Reiter*, Munich, 1912, p. 12

In this era of the great battle for the new art we fight unorganized as *Fauves*, i.e., "wild beasts" against an old established power. The battle seems unequal, but in matters of the spirit it is not numbers that count but the strength of ideas. The most dreaded weapons of the *Fauves* are their new ideas — they are more deadly than steel and capable of breaking what was thought unbreakable.

Franz Marc, "Die 'Wilden' Deutschlands," *Almanach Der Blaue Reiter*, Munich, 1912, p. 6

73   Franz Marc, *Nude with Cat.* 1910

74 Franz Marc, *Grazing Horses II (?)*. 1910

The first signs of new times are very difficult to define, for who can see clearly what they point to and what is to come? But the mere fact that they exist, that they appear today in so many unrelated places, and that they are of such profound truth, entitles us to believe that they are the first signs of the era at hand; that they are beacons which guide the wayfarer.

This is a unique hour — is it too bold to point out these small rare signs of the times?

Franz Marc, "Zwei Bilder," *Almanach Der Blaue Reiter*, Munich, 1912, p. 12

It is remarkable how differently people value spiritual and material goods.

If somebody has conquered a new colony for his country everybody rejoices; there will be not one moment of hesitation before possession is taken of it. Technical inventions are welcomed with the same kind of enthusiasm.

If, however, somebody offers his country a purely spiritual gift it is almost always rejected with agitation and indignation. His gift is regarded with suspicion, and every attempt is made to get rid of it. If it were still permitted, the donor would even today be burned at the stake . . .

This melancholy observation has its place in the columns of the *Almanach Der Blaue Reiter* because it points out a great danger which may bring about the death of the "Blue Riders": people's general lack of interest in new spiritual values.

We see this danger with absolute clarity. Our gifts will be rejected with anger and abuse: "Why new pictures? Why new ideas? What can we buy with that? We've already got too many old ones, forced on us by education and fashion, and we don't enjoy those either."

But perhaps we are right after all. They will not want to but they will have to accept. Because we believe that our world of ideas is not like a house of cards with which we play but that it contains elements of a movement that is today stirring the entire world . . .

Cézanne and El Greco are congenial spirits in spite of the span of time between them, and their works mark the beginning of a new era in painting. They were both aware of what might be called the mystical structure of the inner world, which is the great problem of today's generation.

Franz Marc, "Geistige Güter," *Almanach Der Blaue Reiter*, Munich, 1912, pp. 1–3

75 Franz Marc, *Blue Horse I.* 1911

76   Franz Marc, *Cows (red, green, yellow).* 1912

. . . Marc was then living in a farmhouse in Sindelsdorf (Upper Bavaria, between Murnau and Kochel). We soon became acquainted with him personally and found the outward appearance corresponded perfectly to the inner person; he was a big, broad-shouldered man with a powerful gait, a head that was full of character and an unusual face with features that revealed a rare combination of strength, acuity, and tenderness. In Munich he seemed to be too big, his gait too long. He gave the impression that the city was too small for him, that it "restricted" him. The countryside matched his free nature and I always took a particular delight in seeing him stroll through meadows, fields, and woods with a stick in his hand and a rucksack on his back. The naturalness of his manner corresponded marvelously to these natural surroundings, and nature herself seemed to be pleased with him. This organic bond between him and nature was reflected too in his relationship with his dog "Russi," a large white sheep dog which in manner, strength of character, and mildness of disposition constituted an exact four-legged copy of his master. The Marc-Russi relationship was just one example of Marc's profound, organic relationship with the entire animal world. In his pictures, however, the animals are so closely merged with the landscape that in spite of their "expressiveness," their Marc-like characteristics, they nevertheless always remain simply an organic part of the whole. At that time particularly there were very few people who had any awareness of the whole, and even fewer who experienced this whole in the deepest part of their being, and who were qualified for such an experience. Even today their number is not much greater. For the world is still much too materialistic, that is, the world which is inhabited by present-day man and which he has created himself, unfortunately for him . . .

So Franz Marc was never an "animal painter," nor a "naturalist," nor an "Expressionist," and even less a "Cubist" — all labels which are often pinned on him. In his youth he unconsciously envisaged the idea of a synthesis. In this respect alone he must be considered a "new man." And this was the mutual ground on which we met and on which our plans developed. And thus the "Blue Rider" was born.

Wassily Kandinsky, "Unsere Freundschaft," in Klaus Lankheit, *Franz Marc im Urteil seiner Zeit*, Cologne, 1960, p. 46

... People realized that art is concerned with the mysterious region of deepest thought and feeling and that therefore the rebirth of art cannot be a matter of form but a matter of the mind. Mysticism awoke in the souls of men, and with it primordial elements of art.

It is impossible to explain the latest paintings of the *Fauves* as a result of merely formal developments or as a variation of impressionistic methods ... Those beautiful prismatic colors and that famous Cubism have become meaningless goals for the *Fauves*.

Their ideas were of an altogether different nature. By their work they wanted to create contemporary symbols that would be placed on the altars of the spiritual religion of the future ...

Mockery and miscomprehension will be for them roses in their path.

Franz Marc, "Die 'Wilden' Deutschlands," *Almanach Der Blaue Reiter*, Munich, 1912, p. 6

77   Franz Marc, *Deer in the Forest II.* 1912

78   Franz Marc, *Red and Blue Horses.* 1912

. . . The general public has now reached the point of considering a beautifully painted winter landscape in terms of art, even when the painter does not have the slightest idea of art but simply followed the hastily learned laws of optics and received a little friendly assistance from the camera. People's feelings for form have become so numb and their point of view so hackneyed that they take the most superficial comparison with nature as a usable criterion for art; and their brains have become so lazy that they can no longer tell the difference between art and imitation. Popular art, that is, a feeling on the part of the people for artistic form, can only rise again after the whole ragbag of rotten conceptions of art stemming from the nineteenth century has been eradicated from memory.

From an essay by Franz Marc in *PAN*, 21 March 1912

I have never seen a painter paint with such divine earnestness and gentleness as he did. "Lemon oxen" and "fire buffaloes" he called his animals, and on his temple a star began to gleam. But even the wild animals turn into plants in his tropical hand. Tigresses he transformed magically into anemones, leopards he adorned with gemlike gillyflowers; when the panther leaps on the antelope on the rocks he called it the pure kill. He felt like the young patriarch of Biblical times, a mighty Jacob he, the Lord of Canaan. With furore he fought his way through the thicket. His beautiful face was reflected in the water and many a time he bore his wondrous heart wrapped in hides like a shepherd carrying his sleeping boy home over the fields when he was tired.

That was all before the war.

Else Lasker-Schüler on Franz Marc in Klaus Lankheit, *Franz Marc im Urteil seiner Zeit*, Cologne, 1960, p. 79

79   Franz Marc, *The Tiger.* 1912

80 Franz Marc, *Deer in a Monastery Garden.* 1912

I saw the visual image as seen through the waterhen's eye as it dives: the thousand concentric rings that encircle every little bit of life. I saw the blue of the whispering sky that the lake drinks up; I saw the waterhen surfacing again, rapturously, in a distant spot. Do realize, my friends, what painting is: the surfacing of the image in another place.

Franz Marc, *Briefe, Aufzeichnungen und Aphorismen*, Vol. 1, Berlin, 1920, p. 130, no. 82

All objects have their outer "skin" and their core, their surface and their essence, their façade and their truth. The fact that we can touch only the "skin" without getting to the core, that we can only perceive the surface without feeling the essence, and, finally, that the façade prevents us from discovering the truth: what does this really mean in view of their existential definitiveness?

Franz Marc, *Briefe, Aufzeichnungen und Aphorismen*, Vol. 1, Berlin, 1920, p. 126, no. 1

81   Franz Marc, *In the Rain*. 1912

82   Gabriele Münter, *Kandinsky painting.* 1903

I liked Hüsgen's masks of the "*Scharfrichter*" [execution squad] very much. My fingers started itching — I wanted to do sculpture. Soon I went to the Phalanx School and enrolled for Hüsgen's afternoon sculpture class. K.'s evening life class was part of the course. It was quite a new experience for me because K., quite unlike the other teachers, explained all problems thoroughly and intensely and accepted me as a human being with conscious aspirations and capable of setting herself tasks and aims.

This was something new for me and impressed me.

Undated note by Gabriele Münter, "Blue Rider" Archives, Städtische Galerie, Munich

The earliest paintings date from the year 1904. Although appearing "impressionistic," when compared with her later and most recent work, they reveal the same inner substance. Persistence in expressing the same spiritual values throughout his works is the true and unmistakable proof of the genuine artist, much as the individual work may change its style in the course of time. The application of this criterion is a sure way, in art, of distinguishing the true creator from the fake. It plows a deep furrow between true and pseudo-art, which unfortunately always accompanies every "movement" and is the art world's worst enemy.

From Kandinsky's introduction to an exhibition with works by Gabriele Münter in the Neue Kunstsalon Dietzel, Munich, 1913; "Blue Rider" Archives, Städtische Galerie, Munich

83   Gabriele Münter, *View from a Window in Sèvres*. 1906

84 Gabriele Münter, *Trees in Blossom in Lana*. 1908

It is particularly satisfying to be able to ascertain here that Gabriele Münter's original, profound, one might almost say authentically German talent can under no circumstances be labeled masculine or even as "almost masculine." Her talent — and we take further satisfaction in reemphasizing it — is fundamentally and exclusively feminine.

The moment we enter the small and intimate room of the Neue Kunstsalon we immediately sense the breathing presence of a woman.

It is agreeable to be unable to account for the underlying cause of this feeling. Gabriele Münter does not paint "feminine" subjects, neither does she work with feminine materials nor permit herself any feminine coquetry. There is no evidence of either sentimentality or superficial elegance, or even so-called feminine weakness. On the other hand, we find no masculine mannerisms, that is, no "powerful brushwork" or paint heavily applied to the canvas. The pictures are painted throughout with delicate and precise balance which lacks all — male or female — mannerism and affectation. We are almost inclined to say these pictures are painted with modesty, that is, not with a view to any outward appearance but as a result of an impulse from within.

From Kandinsky's introduction to an exhibition with works by Gabriele Münter in the Neue Kunstsalon Dietzel, Munich, 1913; "Blue Rider" Archives, Städtische Galerie, Munich

We had discovered Murnau on an outing and recommended it to Jawlensky and Werefkin, who then asked us to join them there in the following autumn. We stayed at the Griesbräu and liked it very much.

After a short period of torment I made a great step forward — from painting from nature, more or less impressionistically — to a feeling of content — to abstracting — to rendering something essential.

It was a beautiful, interesting, and happy time with lots of discussions about art with the enthusiastic "Giselists."[1] I particularly liked to show my work to Jawlensky — for one thing he was ready to praise . . . generously; and for another thing he explained many things to me, giving me the benefit of his experience and achievements and talking about "synthesis." A nice colleague! Every one of the four of us worked hard and everyone made good progress. I made masses of studies. There were some days when I painted five studies (on 33 × 41 cm cardboards), some others when I painted only three, and few days when I didn't paint at all . . . We were all very industrious.

Note from Gabriele Münter's diary, May 1911; "Blue Rider" Archives, Städtische Galerie, Munich

[1] Jawlensky and Marianne von Werefkin, because they were living together in an apartment in Giselastrasse, were named the "Giselisten" by their friends.

85   Gabriele Münter, *View of the Murnau Marsh.* 1908

86   Gabriele Münter, *Portrait of Marianne von Werefkin.* 1909

Gabriele Münter has a vision of things quite her own, a sense of humor and of life that penetrates beneath the surface, and that manifests itself in a technic that is, one might say, almost nonchalant.

Arthur Jerome Eddy, *Cubists and Post-Impressionism*, Chicago, 1914, p. 114

If I had set myself any model — as was to some extent the case from 1903–13 — it was probably van Gogh seen with the eyes of Jawlensky and his theories (his talk about synthesis). But that is nothing compared with what Kandinsky meant for me. It was he who cherished, understood, protected, and furthered my talent.

Undated note by Gabriele Münter, "Blue Rider" Archives, Städtische Galerie, Munich

87　Gabriele Münter, *Jawlensky and Werefkin*. About 1908–9

88   Gabriele Münter, *Still Life in Grey.* 1910

You're a hopeless pupil — there's no teaching you anything. You can produce only what has developed in you. Everything comes to you from nature.

Remark by Kandinsky, quoted in Johannes Eichner, *Kandinsky und Gabriele Münter*, Munich, 1957, p. 38

Her artistic aspiration finds its culmination in color, color as deep and glowing as in medieval stained-glass windows; and juxtapositions of color as enchanting as exploding fireworks. The painter's strength lies in her ability to tame the wealth of her colors and create a harmony . . .

Wilhelm Waetzoldt in the *Hamburger Correspondent*, Hamburg, 18 June 1910

89　Gabriele Münter, *Village Street in Winter*. 1911

90   Gabriele Münter, *Man at the dinner Table (portrait of Kandinsky).* 1911

Among these rare artists working in present-day Germany we must include Gabriele Münter. She possesses the following qualities: 1. A precise, discreet, delicate and at the same time boldly distinctive drawing style made up of elements of mischievousness, melancholy, and dreams — truly German characteristics, as can be seen from the work of the old German masters and heard in German folk music and folk poetry. 2. A simple, personal color harmony made up of a few uniformly serious colors whose deep tones blend with the drawing to strike a peaceful chord. One comes across similar color harmonies in old German stained-glass, paintings on glass, and in the work of primitive German masters, for example the "Master of the Life of Mary."

From the German version of Kandinsky's essay, "Om Konstnären," Stockholm, 1916, "Blue Rider" Archives, Städtische Galerie, Munich

The representation of different objects in a still life proportioned according to different scenes, makes it clear that this kind of transposition is not detrimental to a painting but indeed rather helps to create a strong and differentiated resonance, if properly applied.

Wassily Kandinsky, "Über die Formfrage," *Almanach Der Blaue Reiter*, Munich, 1912, p. 98

91   Gabriele Münter, *Still Life with St. George.* 1911

92 Gabriele Münter, *Woman musing.* 1917

Frau Münter is an extremely radical painter, but her temperament is such that she does not thrust her radicalism upon the viewer. She is a Prussian, and can thus help provide us with a different image of the Prussian character than the caricature which is generally bandied about in this country. There is nothing "pushing" about G. Münter, but a great deal of that proud and sensitive state of mind, that bright, firm major key that gives even sadness an upright bearing — in a word something of the classical in Prussian culture. One notices this immediately in some of the earliest paintings, for in spite of their apparently childlike elements their composition is firmly constructed; and there is something lyrical about them . . .

Gregor Paulsson in the *Stockholm Dagblad*, 14 March 1916

Her views of the Alpine countryside are painted, as it were, in deliberate contradiction to the pleasing motif, the pretty view; and thus they produce the essence of its color and atmosphere. They are composed without linear perspective; but the different planes of the paintings freely represent the character of the landscape: the stillness of a winter's day or the intimacy of a village street. Intimate and at the same time boldy conceived, with a clear and simple composition in which the mountains usually reach the sky, these pictures possess that "certain something" which places them above mere studies of nature.

Fritz Nemitz in *Westermanns Monatshefte*, 1949, issue 7, p. 56

93   Gabriele Münter, *View of the Mountains.* 1934

94   Gabriele Münter, *Peonies and orange Lily.* 1956

There was nothing in the family heritage that would explain Gabriele Münter's talent and there was nobody to discover or to encourage it in her early youth. Like some hidden gift from nature, her ability to create something in the field of the visual arts was unknown to herself and to her family. As a girl she would very casually use her talent and only comparatively late in life did she begin to develop it more or less systematically. But from the very outset there was a strength of character that prevented her from wasting her natural endowment in mechanical perfection and that, at the same time, was decisive for her development as an artist. Her personality did not depend on others; she fiercely rejected prejudice and convention in all its manifestations, and in her naïveté she cared only for things human and simple.

Johannes Eichner, *Kandinsky und Gabriele Münter*, Munich, 1957, p. 26

Small wonder that Franz Marc should have liked Niestlé. They not only shared a love for animals but, even more, they shared the intensive study of animal behavior and the complete lack of sentimentality in representing them. Much as Marc's and Niestlé's forms differ from each other, their paintings have in common the artist's emotional sympathy with his subject.

Scientifically exact drawings like Audubon's birds of America or Niestlé's paintings need not necessarily be unartistic. In spite of the strictly accurate detail, Niestlé's paintings represent a whole and sound world.

H.K.R.

95   Jean Bloé Niestlé, *Water Pipit.* 1909

96   Jean Bloé Niestlé, *Migrating Starlings.* 1910

He is a very shy, very young French artist and is possessed by such a melancholy that it makes you suffer with him when you see his drawings . . . . Technically they remind me of the Japanese but Niestlé is deeper in feeling and what is even more miraculous, even more precise . . . He has just finished something incredible: a long strip of paper — two meters — with a flock of one hundred starlings in flight. You think you hear the sound of their moving wings and their twittering. And they are all different; each of the birds has an individual character.

From a letter from Franz Marc about Niestlé, 20 October 1905

Is there a more intriguing idea for an artist than to imagine the way that nature can be seen through the eye of an animal? How does a horse see the world? Or an eagle, or a deer, or a dog? How poor and soulless is the conventional way of setting animals into a landscape as we see it; we should rather try to immerse ourselves in the animals' souls in order to enable us to discover the images they see.

Franz Marc, *Briefe, Aufzeichnungen und Aphorismen*, Vol. 1, Berlin, 1920, p. 121

97   Jean Bloé Niestlé, *Cat on the Prowl.* 1910

98   Arnold Schönberg, *Red Eyes*. About 1910

Applying this criterion to Schönberg's pictures we see immediately
that here we are dealing with painting, whether it be outside the
mainstream of the great contemporary movement or not.

In every one of Schönberg's pictures we find the artist's inner
desire expressed in an appropriate form. In his painting as well as
in his music (insofar as I can speak about it as a layman) Schönberg
rejects the superfluous (that is, the detrimental) and goes straight
for the essential (that is, the necessary). He discards any kind of
"embellishment" or refinement.

His *Self-portrait* is painted with the scrapings left on the palette.
And what better material could he have chosen to achieve this strong,
sober, and precise impression?

A portrait of a lady has more or less no "color" at all, apart from
the sickly pink of the dress. A landscape is grey-green, nothing but
grey-green. The drawing is simple and really "clumsy." A painting
called *A Vision* consists simply of a head on a very small canvas
(or on a piece of cardboard). The only strong expressive features are
the red-rimmed eyes.

The best name I can think of to describe Schönberg's painting is
"purely painting" [*Nurmalerei*].

Schönberg reproaches himself with his "lack of technique."

I should like to change this self-reproach in accordance with the
criterion previously referred to: Schönberg is wrong — he is not
dissatisfied with his technique but with his inner desire, with his soul,
of which he demands more than it is capable of giving at this moment.

I wish every artist had this same sense of dissatisfaction at all
times.

It is not hard to get on materially. It is not easy to make progress
in the spiritual field.

Kandinsky, *Arnold Schönberg*, Munich, 1912, p. 63

There is one thing my nature cannot stand and that is slavery. Nothing and nobody has any right to own me. When I want to, I give myself freely and without hesitation. But the hand that tries to hold me I sink my teeth into. Freedom is the root of my self. Freely I serve. I am free and pure in the deepest part of my being. Rigid form makes life congeal and halts the movement. Feelings and thoughts are continually in flux. And movement is the essence of life. I am continually on call in the service of what is my only truth — art, the essence, the meaning, the goal, and the basis of life. Accordingly I turn into art everything around me, everything that moves me. Every one of my feelings I hurl into the arena for the artistic triumph of life and of activity. Anyone who fights alongside me has only one enemy — banality. The banner beneath which we stand on every field of battle is always the same — it is the banner of beauty. The bitterer the struggle, the greater my powers and the bigger I myself become, because what I give in terms of idealism accrues to me in realism. It makes my wishes and thoughts and aims and aspirations come true. The ideal, the God in me, must triumph. That is my life's work, certain and strong. In this I am altogether great and true. I am the strong maiden who is loved in battle, not the one who is protected and treated with tenderness. This is glory, but it is also cold. Love without tenderness. Toil without rest. A very beautiful life, but also very much a superhuman one. And I am after all only a woman — more than that, a child. A little bit of tenderness! But I shall never deny the beauty within me for that alone is truth. This thirst for tenderness is not truth, it is falsehood. I must remain myself until the end, so that I may one day die a tranquil death. With my own hand I tear out the little white flower that has taken root in my heart. It leaves behind a drop of blood. I offer up the little white flower in the spacious temple of my thoughts. There it will never wither and die. There in the brilliant light of the ideal it will remain forever white. And I take up my life again . . .

Marianne von Werefkin, *Briefe an einen Unbekannten*, Cologne, 1960, p. 15

99   Marianne von Werefkin, *Self-portrait I*. About 1908

100   Marianne von Werefkin, *Interior with seated Couple*. About 1910

The more reality has been transformed in a work of art into the unreal, the greater the work. The person who can transform a visible impression into a song of color is a master of vision. The person who, by the simple means of color, can turn a visible impression into the realization of his thoughts is master of himself. That is the way artists and their works must be judged.

Marianne von Werefkin, *Briefe an einen Unbekannten*, Cologne, 1960, p. 42

GMS: Abbreviation for "Gabriele Münter Stiftung" (Bequest)

NKVM: Abbreviation for *Neue Künstlervereinigung München*

G: Abbreviation for *Gemälde* (painting), followed by the inventory number of the Städtische Galerie

Erma Barrera-Bossi

Born 1885, lives in Milan. A member of the NKVM who took part in the three NKVM exhibitions in Munich.

Interior with Lamp. 1909

Oil on cardboard, 23.5 × 32.6 cm.
From Gabriele Münter's collection.
Inv. No. GMS 673
Plate 4

Portrait of Marianne von Werefkin (?). About 1910

Oil on cardboard, 71 × 57 cm.
On permanent loan from the Gabriele Münter and Johannes Eichner Foundation

Paul Baum

Born 22 September 1859 in Meissen, died 18 May 1932 in San Gimignano. Studied at the academies in Dresden and Weimar and took part in the first NKVM exhibition. According to a letter from Kandinsky dated 9 December 1909, his paintings appeared in such an unfavorable light among the works of the other participants that Baum wanted to withdraw them. Kandinsky, however, asked him to leave his works until the end of the exhibition. In the first edition of the catalog three works are listed, one of which is illustrated. In the second edition Baum is no longer mentioned, but the illustration, evidently by mistake, is still included. In 1918–21 he was professor for landscape painting at the Academy of Art in Cassel. He lived in San Gimignano from 1924 until his death.

Village Street. About 1910

Oil on canvas, 50.5 × 62.5 cm, signed: Baum.
On permanent loan from the Gabriele Münter and Johannes Eichner Foundation.

Wladimir von Bechtejeff

Born 16 April 1878 in Moscow, lives there. Attended the military academy and left the army with the rank of lieutenant. In about 1902 he moved to Munich on the advice of Jawlensky and studied under Knirr. He became friends with Alexander von Salzmann and Erbslöh. Around 1904–6 he visited Italy, Sicily, and Tunis. He belonged to the NKVM, taking part in its three exhibitions in Munich, and became a member of the *Münchener Neue Sezession* (New Munich Secession). He returned to Russia in 1914 and joined the army. During the revolution he was active on the Committee for Art in Moscow. In 1941 he was evacuated to Kazakhstan. He has illustrated more than 120 books since his return to Russia, and had an important one-man show in 1970 in Moscow.

Porte de France, Tunis. About 1906

Oil on cardboard, 37 × 51 cm, signed: W. Bechtejeff.
Inv. No. G 13183
Plate 2

Small Garden with Trees. About 1906

Oil on cardboard, 34.5 × 40.5 cm.
Inv. No. G 13184

Beach. About 1910

Crayon on paper, 12 × 16 cm.
From Gabriele Münter's collection.
Inv. No. GMS 671

The Tamer of Horses [Rossebändiger].
About 1912

Oil on canvas, 110 × 94 cm, signed: WB.
On permanent loan from the Gabriele Münter and
Johannes Eichner Foundation.
Plate 1

The River Istra. 1960

Oil on canvas, 97.5 × 72 cm, signed: WB 1960.
Inv. No. G 13481

Albert Bloch

Born 2 August 1882 in St. Louis, Missouri, died
9 December 1961 in Lawrence, Kansas. Studied at
the School of Fine Arts, Washington, University,
St. Louis; subsequently went to New York where
he produced illustrations and cartoons for news-
papers. He moved to Munich in 1908, and in 1909
visited Paris. Six of his paintings were included in
the first "Blue Rider" exhibition in Munich,
1911/12, and eight studies in the second. In 1921
he returned to the United States. He taught at the
Art Institute in Chicago, in 1922–3, then became
professor and later director of the Department of
Drawing and Painting at the University of Kansas.
He resigned in 1955.

The Boxing Match. 1912–13

Oil on canvas, 100 × 64 cm, signed: AB (joined);
(on the back): begun XI 1912 / finished X 1913.
Formerly in the collection of Arthur Jerome Eddy,
Chicago. Donated by Gabriele Münter.
Inv. No. G 13484
Plate 3

The Burial. 1914

Oil on canvas, 70 × 100 cm,
signed: AB (joined); (on the back): 1914.
Formerly in the collection of Arthur Jerome Eddy,
Chicago. Donated by Gabriele Münter.
Inv. No. G 13485

Arabesque. 1913

Etching, 17.2 × 12.9 cm, signed: AB (joined) 1913.
From Gabriele Münter's collection.
Inv. No. GMS 672

The Hand of the Entente. About 1916

Pen on paper, 38 × 25.5 cm.
Inv. No. G 172

David Burljuk

Born 22 July 1882 in Kharkov, Russia, died 15 January 1967 in Southampton, New York. Studied
in Odessa and then, in the first years of this century, with W. Diez, Archipoff and Azbé in Munich,
and in 1904 with Cormons in Paris. He met Kandinsky in Odessa in 1910. He belonged to the
Russian *Fauves,* and wrote an article about them
in the *Almanach Der Blaue Reiter.* Two of his
paintings were included in the first "Blue Rider"
exhibition. He went to Russia in 1917, and spent
1920–2 in Japan. From 1922 he lived in the USA.

Still Life with Mask. About 1906

Oil on canvas, 60 × 68 cm.
Formerly in the collection of Michail Larionoff.
Inv. No. G 12760

Wladimir Burljuk

Born 15 March 1886 in Kherson, Russia, died in
action 1917 in Salonica. Attended an art school in
Kasan with his brother David. He studied with
Azbé in Munich in 1903 and went to Paris in 1904.
He subsequently returned to Russia and met Kan-
dinsky in Odessa, 1910. He took part in the NKVM
exhibition in Munich, 1910, and in 1911 in the first
"Blue Rider" exhibition. He exhibited in Herwarth
Walden's first German *Herbstsalon* in Berlin in
1913.

A Dancer (Spring). About 1910

(attributed)
Oil on canvas, 100 × 61 cm.
Inv. No. G 12532
Plate 5

Heinrich Campendonk

Born 3 November 1889 in Krefeld, Germany, died 9 May 1957 in Amsterdam. Studied with Thorn-Prikker at the School for Arts and Crafts in Krefeld. He moved to Sindelsdorf, Upper Bavaria, in October 1911 at the suggestion of Franz Marc. Two of his paintings were included in the first "Blue Rider" exhibition. From 1916 he was in Seeshaupt on the Starnberger See, and in 1920 in Italy. He returned to Krefeld in 1922. In 1926 he became professor at the Academy in Düsseldorf, and was dismissed by the Nazis in 1933. He then went to Belgium, and in 1935 became professor at the National Academy of Fine Arts in Amsterdam.

Female Nude with Cat. 1912

Colored woodcut, 32 × 43.5 cm,
signed: H. Campendonk 1912.
Inv. No. 12696

Women with Masks. 1913

Watercolor, 54.5 × 43 cm,
signed: Campendonk 1913.
Inv. No. G 12822

Girl playing a Shawm. 1914

Oil on canvas, 54 × 32 cm
Inv. No. G 12821
Plate 6

Leopard (Tiger). 1916

Woodcut on Japanese paper, 25.1 × 32 cm,
signed: Campendonk.
Inv. No. G 12799

Seated Girl with Deer. 1916

Woodcut, 43 × 31.5 cm.
Inv. No. G 12661

Seated Woman with Pony. 1916

Woodcut on Japanese paper, 17 × 21.6 cm.
From Gabriele Münter's collection.
Inv. No. GMS 674

The Return. 1919

Lithograph, 28 × 23 cm.
In *Münchner Blätter für Dichtung und Graphik,*
1919, p. 18.
Inv. No. G 13155

Self-portrait. 1919

Woodcut, 28 × 23 cm.
In *Münchner Blätter für Dichtung und Graphik,*
1919, p. 79.
Inv. No. G 13155

The Event. 1920

Woodcut colored by hand, 31.9 × 24.9 cm,
signed: Campendonk.
Donated by Gabriele Münter.
Inv. Nr. G 13103

Portrait of Jean Bloé Niestlé. 1921

Woodcut colored by hand, 45.7 × 40.2 cm,
signed: Campendonk.
Donated by Gabriele Münter.
Inv. No. G 13104

Robert Delaunay

Born 12 April 1885 in Paris, died 25 October 1941 in Montpellier. Began his career as a decorator. He exhibited from 1910 in the *Salon de la Société des Artistes Indépendants.* Four of his paintings and one drawing were included in the first "Blue Rider" exhibition and one drawing in the second. In 1912 Franz Marc and August Macke visited him in Paris. After a meeting with Klee in Paris, Klee translated Delaunay's "De la lumière." He exhibited in Cologne in 1913. He spent 1914–20 in Spain and Portugal, and afterwards went to Paris.

The Eiffel Tower. 1911

Pencil on paper, 24.6 × 16.2 cm,
signed on the back: r. delaunay, paris 1911.
From Gabriele Münter's collection.
Inv. No. GMS 675

Fenêtre sur la ville. 1914

Wax painting on cardboard, 24,8 × 20 cm,
signed: r. delaunay.
On permanent loan from the Gabriele Münter and
Johannes Eichner Foundation.
Plate 7

Emy Dresler

Born 20 December 1880 in Siegen, Germany, died
there 11 May 1962. Studied with Maria Giesler in
Siegen. She visited Kandinsky with her teacher at
the beginning of this century. She met Rudolf Steiner in 1908. In 1910–13 she painted the scenery for
the Anthroposophical Mystery Plays in Munich.
From 1914 she executed wood carvings to Dr. Steiner's instructions at the Goetheanum in Dornach.
She founded a branch of the Anthroposophical Society in Siegen in 1925 and lived by Lake Con-
stance during the Second World War.

Children Playing. About 1907

Tempera on cardboard, 40 × 35 cm.
From Gabriele Münter's collection.
Inv. No. GMS 740

Wilhelm Hüsgen

Born 22 October 1877 in Barmen, Germany, died
19 February 1962 in Munich. Self-taught. With
Kandinsky he founded the artists' union, "Phalanx," where he taught until 1903 and where he became Gabriele Münter's first teacher. He was a
member of the "11 Scharfrichter" (Execution
Squad), a famous Munich cabaret. He lived in
Breslau in 1908–9, in Berlin from 1909–15, and returned to Munich in 1916.

Portrait of Frank Wedekind. 1901

Bronze relief, 33 × 26 cm, signed: Hüsgen.
Inv. No. G 13279

Herr Wind. About 1903

Bronze relief, 32 × 28.5 cm, signed: Hüsgen.
Inv. No. G 13244

Large female Torso. 1908

Bronze, 48 cm high, signed: Hüsgen.
Inv. No. G 12291

Standing Deer. 1916

Bronze, 42.5 × 30.5 cm, signed: Hüsgen.
Inv. No. G 4168

Alexej von Jawlensky

Born 13 March 1864 in Kuzlovo, Russia, died
15 March 1941 in Wiesbaden. After leaving the
military academy with the rank of lieutenant, he
was stationed in 1884 in Moscow and in 1889 in
St. Petersburg, where he studied painting at the
same time at the Academy with Rjepin. He left the
army in 1896 with the rank of captain and went to
Munich with Marianne von Werefkin. There he
studied with Azbé and became friends with Kandinsky. He first went to Paris in 1903; he met
Matisse in 1905 and studied with him in 1907. He
became a member of the NKVM in 1909 and took
part in all three exhibitions. He was invited to
participate in the "Blue Rider" exhibition organized by the *Sturm,* 1913, and became a member of
the *Münchener Neue Sezession.* In 1914 he went to
Saint-Prex on the Lake of Geneva and in 1917 to
Zürich. He lived in Wiesbaden from 1921 until his
death. With Kandinsky, Klee, and Feininger, he
became one of the "Blue Four" in 1924.

Hyacinth. 1902

Oil on canvas, 55.5 × 34.8 cm,
signed: A. Jawlensky.
Donated by Gabriele Münter.
Inv. No. G 13106

The Hunchbacked Man. 1905

Oil on cardboard, 52.5 × 49.5 cm,
signed: A. Jawlensky.
Donated by Gabriele Münter.
Inv. No. G 13107
Plate 8

Füssen. 1905

Oil on cardboard, 38 × 50 cm,
signed: A. Jawlensky.
On permanent loan from the Gabriele Münter and
Johannes Eichner Foundation.

View of Wasserburg. 1906

Oil on cardboard, 30.9 × 47.8 cm,
signed: A. Jawlensky/1906.
Donated by Gabriele Münter.
Inv. No. G 13108

Street in Winter. About 1906–7

Oil on cardboard, 68.5 × 49.8 cm.
From Gabriele Münter's collection.
Inv. No. GMS 679

Summer Evening in Murnau. 1908

Oil on cardboard, 33.2 × 45.1 cm,
signed: A. Jawlensky.
Donated by Gabriele Münter.
Inv. No. G 13109

Sketch of a Street in Murnau. About 1908–9

Oil on cardboard, 33.3 × 41.3 cm.
From Gabriele Münter's collection.
Inv. No. GMS 677

Landscape near Murnau. 1909

Oil on cardboard, 50.5 × 54.5 cm,
signed: A. Jawlensky — 09.
From Gabriele Münter's collection.
Inv. No. GMS 678
Plate 9

Portrait of the Dancer Alexander Sacharov. 1909

Oil on cardboard, 69.5 × 66.5 cm.
Formerly in the collection of Clotilde von Derp-Sacharov.
Inv. No. G 13388
Plate 11

Seated female Nude. About 1910

Oil on cardboard, 70 × 42 cm,
signed: A. Jawlensky.
Inv. No. G 12476
Plate 10

Still Life with Fruit. About 1910

Oil on cardboard, 48 × 67.7 cm,
signed: A. Jawlensky.
From Gabriele Münter's collection.
Inv. No. GMS 680
Plate 12

Maturity. About 1912

Oil on cardboard, 53.5 × 49.5 cm,
signed: A. Jawlensky.
Inv. No. G 13000
Plate 13

Head of a Woman. 1912

Lithograph, 55 × 43 cm, signed: A. Jawlensky.
Donated by Gabriele Münter.
Inv. No. G 13110

Portrait of Kandinsky. About 1912

Pencil, 22.5 × 28.8 cm.
From Gabriele Münter's collection.
Inv. No. GMS 681

Spanish Lady. 1913

Oil on cardboard, 67 × 48.5 cm,
signed: A. Jawlensky/13.
Inv. No. G 12556
Plate 14

Reclining Nude. About 1913–14

Pencil, 48.3 × 62 cm, signed: A. Jawlensky.
Inv. No. G 12963

Meditation. 1918

Oil on cardboard, 40 × 31 cm,
signed: A. Jawlensky.
Bernhard Koehler Bequest 1965.
Inv. No. G 13340
Plate 15

Meditation, "The Prayer." 1922

Oil on cardboard, 40 × 30 cm, signed: A. J.
Bernhard Koehler Bequest 1965.
Inv. No. G 13341
Plate 16

Meditation on a gold background. 1936

Oil on paper, 14 × 11 cm, signed: A. J. 36.
Bernhard Koehler Bequest 1965.
Inv. No. G 13339
Plate 17

Andreas Jawlensky

Born 18 January 1902 in Ansback, near Preli,
Latvia, lives in Locarno, Switzerland. Son of
Alexej von Jawlensky. He grew up in Giselastrasse, Munich, and learned painting from his
father. He spent 1914–16 in Saint-Prex on the Lake
of Geneva, where he met Hodler, 1917 in Zürich,
1918–22 in Ascona, and 1922–40 in Wiesbaden. In
1941 he was Russian interpreter in the German
army and was a prisoner of war in the Soviet
Union from 1945 until 1955. He moved to Locarno
in 1957.

Red Flowers on a pink Table. About 1912

Oil on cardboard, 49.5 × 53.5 cm, signed and veri-
fied on the back by Andreas Jawlensky.
From Gabriele Münter's collection.
Inv. No. GMS 682

Eugen von Kahler

Born 6 January 1882 in Prague, died there 13 December 1911. First drawing lessons with A. Jakesch
in Prague. From 1901–5 he was in Munich, first at
Knirr's school and then in Stuck's painting class at
the Academy. He later studied privately with
Hugo von Habermann. Early in 1906 he was in
Berlin, and afterwards in Paris until the end of
1907. He spent the winter of 1907–8 in Egypt,

1908–9 in Brussels, and 1909–10 in North Africa
and Spain. He was in London in early 1910 and
then moved to Munich. Two of his "drawings"
(probably the ones listed here) were included in the
first "Blue Rider" exhibition.

The Garden of Love. About 1910–11

Mixed media, 19 × 27.1 cm.
From Gabriele Münter's collection.
Inv. No. GMS 684
Plate 18

Bathers. About 1910–11

Mixed media, 18 × 22.2 cm.
From Gabriele Münter's collection.
Inv. No. GMS 683

Wassily Kandinsky

Born 5 December 1866 in Moscow, died 13 December 1944 in Paris. He studied law and social
sciences in Moscow. In 1896 he declined a professorship at the university at Dorpat. In 1897 he
went to Munich, where he studied art with Azbé
and later with Stuck at the Academy. He founded
the artists' union, "Phalanx," in 1901, and taught at
its private art school until 1903. He spent 1904–8
traveling with Gabriele Münter in Europe and
North Africa, and in 1908 returned to Munich. In
1909 he was co-founder of the NKVM, but withdrew in 1911 with Marc, Münter, and Kubin. In
the first "Blue Rider" exhibition in 1911 he showed
three paintings and a number of paintings on glass
not listed in the catalog; in the second exhibition
twelve of his watercolors were included. The
Almanach Der Blaue Reiter was published in 1912.
In 1914 Kandinsky went to Switzerland and then
returned to Russia. He was in Stockholm from the
end of 1915 until 1916. He married Nina Andre-
jewsky in 1917. In 1918 he became a member of
the art staff at the People's Commissariat for the
Arts and teacher at the Institute for the Decorative
Arts in Moscow, and in 1919 director of the State
Museum of Painting. From 1919 to 1921 he reorga-
nized more than thirty museums. In 1920 he became professor of art theory at the university in
Moscow. He returned to Germany at the end of

1921. He was professor at the Bauhaus, first in Weimar and subsequently in Dessau, from 1922 until the closing of the Bauhaus by the Nazis in 1933, when he moved to Paris. He took part in the activities of the "abstraction-création" group. He became a Frenchman in 1939.

Waterfall I (Kesselberg Falls near Kochel). About 1900

Oil on canvas board, 32.4 × 23.5 cm, signed: Kandinsky.
Inv. No. GMS 4

Landscape with Knights. 1900

Tempera on paper, 20 × 23 cm, signed (on mount): Kandinsky (in Russian characters) 900.
Inv. No. GMS 619

Weir. 1901

Oil on cardboard, 32 × 24 cm, signed: Kandinsky.
Inv. No. GMS 3

Nikolaiplatz in Munich-Schwabing. About 1901

Oil on canvas board, 23.7 × 32.2 cm, signed: Kandinsky.
Inv. No. GMS 2

Gabriele Münter in Kochel. 1902

Oil on canvas board, 32.7 × 23.9 cm, signed: Kandinsky.
Inv. No. GMS 9

Kochel am See. About 1902

Oil on canvas board, 24 × 32.9 cm, signed: Kandinsky.
Inv. No. GMS 8

Kochelsee with red House. About 1902

Oil on canvas board, 32 × 23.8 cm, signed: Kandinsky.
Inv. No. GMS 12

In the Park. About 1902

Tempera on tinted paper, 45.6 × 94.5 cm.
Inv. No. GMS 612

Mountain Landscape with Lake. About 1902

Oil on canvas, 28 × 76 cm.
Inv. No. GMS 642

The Wedding Procession. About 1902

(The Young Couple)
Tempera on tinted paper, 41 × 56,8 cm, signed: Kandinsky.
Inv. No. GMS 90

Russian Knight. 1902

Tempera on paper, 12.8 × 29.4 cm, signed: Kandinsky.
Inv. No. GMS 622

Dusk. About 1902

Tempera on cardboard, 15.6 × 47.5 cm, signed: Kandinsky.
Inv. No. GMS 99

Autumn Study — Russia. About 1902

Oil on canvas board, 23.7 × 32.7 cm, signed: Kandinsky.
Inv. No. GMS 10

The Isar (near Grosshesselohe). About 1902

Oil on canvas board, 32.5 × 23.6 cm, signed: Kandinsky.
Inv. No. GMS 7

Englischer Garten in Munich. About 1902

Oil on canvas board, 23.7 × 32.3 cm, signed: Kandinsky.
Inv. No. GMS 11

Waterfall II (near Kochel). About 1902

Oil on canvas board, 33 × 23.9 cm.
Inv. No. GMS 25

Near Starnberg. About 1902

Oil on canvas board, 23.7 × 32.3 cm, signed: Kandinsky.
Inv. No. GMS 6

Knight on Horseback. About 1902–3

Oil on canvas, 108 × 160 cm.
Inv. No. GMS 1

Old City. 1903

Tempera on cardboard, 29.7 × 53 cm,
signed: Kandinsky.
Inv. No. GMS 89

Gabriele Münter painting in Kallmünz I. 1903

Oil on canvas board, 23.7 × 32.7 cm.
Inv. No. GMS 5

Gabriele Münter painting in Kallmünz II. 1903

Oil on canvas, 58.5 × 58.5 cm.
Inv. No. GMS 14
Plate 20

Study for the yellow Stagecoach. 1903

Oil on canvas board, 23.5 × 32.7 cm.
Inv. No. GMS 13

Landscape with a yellow Field. About 1903

Oil on cardboard, 29.8 × 44.5 cm.
Inv. No. GMS 19

Landscape with Castle. About 1903

Oil on canvas board, 23.8 × 33 cm.
Inv. No. GMS 15

In the Forest. About 1903

Tempera on wood, 26 × 19.8 cm,
signed: Kandinsky.
From the collection of Jawlensky.
Inv. No. G 12771

Couple on Horseback. About 1903

Oil on canvas, 55 × 50.5 cm, signed: Kandinsky.
Inv. No. GMS 26
Plate 19

Sunday. 1904

Oil on canvas, 38.5 × 89 cm.
Inv. No. GMS 613

Night. 1904

Tempera on tinted paper: 33.8 × 33.7 cm,
signed: Kandinsky.
Inv. No. GMS 583

Once upon a Time. 1904

Tempera on tinted paper, 35.3 × 19.9 cm,
signed: (on the mount): Kandinsky.
Inv. No. GMS 96

Evening. About 1904

Tempera on tinted paper, 21.1 × 32 cm.
Inv. No. GMS 184

Dialogue. About 1904

Tempera on cardboard, 40.6 × 30.8 cm,
signed: (on the mount): Kandinsky.
Inv. No. GMS 97

Spring. About 1904

Tempera on tinted paper, 27.6 × 33.7 cm,
signed: Kandinsky.
Inv. No. GMS 87

Beach Chairs in Holland. 1904

Oil on canvas board, 24 × 32.6 cm,
signed: Kandinsky.
Inv. No. GMS 16
Plate 21

View from the Hotel Saint-Georges, Tunis. 1905

Oil on canvas board, 23.7 × 32.2 cm.
Inv. No. GMS 18

Carthage. 1905

Oil on canvas board, 23.6 × 32.8 cm.
Inv. No. GMS 17

Country Road. 1905

Tempera on black paper, 33.4 × 50.7 cm,
signed (on the back): Kandinsky.
Inv. No. GMS 98

Negroes at Work. 1905

Tempera on cardboard, 39.5 × 50 cm,
signed: Kandinsky.
Inv. No. GMS 91

Street Scene in an African Town. 1905

Tempera on tinted paper, 16.7 × 26.8 cm.
Inv. No. GMS 100

Arabian Street, Evening. 1905

Tempera on black paper, 25 × 17.7 cm.
Inv. No. GMS 103

Arabian Horsemen. 1905

Tempera on black paper, 28.7 × 41.5 cm,
signed: Kandinsky.
Inv. No. GMS 95

Portrait of Gabriele Münter. 1905

Oil on canvas, 45 × 45 cm, signed: K-Y.
Inv. No. GMS 30
Plate 22

Landscape with a Russian Beauty. About 1905

Tempera on black paper, 41.4 × 28.7 cm.
Inv. No. GMS 92

A Russian Legend. About 1905–6

Tempera on canvas, 16.8 × 24.5 cm.
Inv. No. GMS 93

Bay of Rapallo. 1906

Oil on canvas board, 23.9 × 33 cm.
Inv. No. GMS 20

Santa Margherita. 1906

Oil on canvas board, 23.7 × 32.7 cm.
Inv. No. GMS 21

Rapallo — a View from the Window. 1906

Oil on cardboard, 23.8 × 33 cm.
Inv. No. GMS 22

Near Paris. 1906

Oil on canvas board, 23.7 × 32.7 cm.
Inv. No. GMS 27

In the Parc de Saint-Cloud. 1906

Oil on canvas board, 23.6 × 32.7 cm.
Inv. No. GMS 23

Sèvres. 1906

Oil on canvas board, 23 × 32 cm.
Inv. No. GMS 24

Night. 1906–7

Tempera on tinted paper, 29.8 × 49.7 cm,
signed: Kandinsky.
Inv. No. GMS 88
Plate 23

Panic. 1907

Tempera on black paper, 50.1 × 36.2 cm.
Inv. No. GMS 94

Autumn Study near Oberau. 1908

Oil on cardboard, 32.8 × 44.5 cm,
signed: Kandinsky.
Inv. No. GMS 28

Village. 1908
(Study for *Landscape with Tree Trunk, Murnau
from the West*).

Oil on cardboard, 32.5 × 44.2 cm,
signed: Kandinsky.
Inv. No. GMS 31

Street in Murnau. 1908

Oil on cardboard, 32.8 × 40.7 cm.
Inv. No. GMS 32

View over the Staffelsee. 1908

Oil on cardboard, 32.7 × 40.5 cm.
Inv. No. GMS 33

View from the Griesbräu (Murnau). 1908

Oil on cardboard, 49.8 × 69.6 cm.
Inv. No. GMS 34

Outskirts of Munich. 1908

Oil on cardboard, 68.8 × 49 cm,
signed: Kandinsky 1908.
Inv. No. GMS 35

Snowladen Trees in Kochel. 1909

Oil on cardboard, 32.8 × 44.5 cm.
Inv. No. GMS 38

Cemetery and Vicarage in Kochel. 1909

Oil on cardboard, 44.4 × 32.7 cm,
signed: Kandinsky.
Inv. No. GMS 43

Cemetery in Kochel. 1909

Oil on cardboard, 32.9 × 44.6 cm.
Inv. No. GMS 39

Houses in Murnau. 1909

Oil on cardboard, 32.7 × 44.5 cm,
signed: Kandinsky.
Inv. No. GMS 36

Study of Nature in Murnau I. 1909

Oil on cardboard, 32.9 × 44.6 cm.
Inv. No. GMS 45

Study of Nature in Murnau II. 1909

Oil on cardboard, 32.8 × 44.5 cm.
Inv. No. GMS 44

Study of Nature in Murnau III. 1909

Oil on cardboard, 31.5 × 44.7 cm,
signed: Kandinsky.
Inv. No. GMS 40

Study of Nature in Murnau IV. 1909

Oil on cardboard, 32.7 × 40.2 cm,
signed: Kandinsky.
Inv. No. GMS 37

Murnau with Rainbow. 1909

Oil on cardboard, 32.8 × 42.8 cm,
signed: Kandinsky.
Inv. No. GMS 41

Grüngasse, Murnau. 1909

Oil on cardboard, 33 × 44.6 cm.
Inv. No. GMS 42
Plate 24

Railroad near Murnau. 1909

Oil on cardboard, 36 × 49 cm.
Inv. No. GMS 49

Horses. 1909

Oil on canvas, 97 × 107.3 cm,
signed: Kandinsky 1909.
Inv. No. GMS 53

The yellow Horse. About 1909

Painting on glass, 15.9 × 28.8 cm, signed (on the
back, by Gabriele Münter): Kandinsky, erstes Glas-
bild.
Inv. No. GMS 117

Bedroom at 36 Ainmillerstrasse, Munich. 1909

Oil on cardboard, 48.5 × 69.5 cm,
signed: Kandinsky 1909.
Inv. No. GMS 51

Living Room at 36 Ainmillerstrasse, Munich.
About 1909

Oil on cardboard, 50 × 65 cm, signed: Kandinsky.
Inv. No. GMS 52

Mountain. 1909

Oil on canvas, 109 × 109 cm,
signed: Kandinsky 1909.
Inv. No. GMS 54
Plate 25

Oriental Scene [Orientalisches]. 1909

Oil on cardboard, 69.5 × 96.5 cm.
Inv. No. GMS 55

Improvisation 6 [Afrikanisches]. 1909

Oil on canvas, 107×95.5 cm,
signed: Kandinsky 1909.
Inv. No. GMS 56
Plate 26

Study for Improvisation 2 (Funeral March). 1909

Oil on cardboard, 50×69.5 cm.
Inv. No. GMS 50

All Saints I. About 1909–10

Oil on cardboard, 50×64.5 cm,
signed with monogram.
Inv. No. GMS 71

Study for Autumn I. 1910

Oil on cardboard, 33×45 cm, signed: Kandinsky.
Inv. No. GMS 48

Mountain Landscape with Church. 1910

Oil on cardboard, 32.7×44.8 cm,
signed: Kandinsky.
Inv. No. GMS 46

A Lady (portrait of Gabriele Münter). 1910

Oil on canvas, 110×109 cm,
signed: Kandinsky 1910.
Inv. No. GMS 29

Impression (Sunday) 1910

Oil on canvas, 107.5×95 cm,
signed (on the back): Kandinsky.
Inv. No. GMS 57

The Cow. 1910

Oil on canvas, 95.5×105 cm,
signed: Kandinsky 1910.
Inv. No. GMS 58

Church in Murnau. 1910

Oil on cardboard, 64.7×50.2 cm.
Inv. No. GMS 59

Garden. 1910

Oil on canvas, 66×82 cm,
signed: Kandinsky 1910.
Inv. No. GMS 60
Plate 27

Study for Winter 2. About 1910

Oil on cardboard, 33×44.7 cm, signed: Kandinsky.
Inv. No. GMS 47

Study of Nature in Murnau V. About 1910

Oil on cardboard, 32×44 cm.
Inv. No. GMS 61

Last Supper. About 1910

Painting on glass, 23.3×34.2 cm,
signed (on the back, by Gabriele Münter):
Kandinsky 1909 oder 1910.
Inv. No. GMS 111

Study for a Last Supper. About 1910

Painting on glass, 9×7 cm.
Inv. No. GMS 114

Improvisation 18 (with Tombstones). 1911

Oil on canvas, 141×120 cm,
signed: Kandinsky 1911.
Inv. No. GMS 77

Romantic Landscape. 1911

Oil on canvas, 94.3×129 cm,
signed: Kandinsky 1911.
Inv. No. GMS 83
Plate 28

Improvisation 19. 1911

Oil on canvas, 120×141.5 cm,
signed (on the back): Kandinsky.
Inv. No. GMS 79
Plate 29

Improvisation 19a. 1911

Oil on canvas, 97×106 cm.
Inv. No. GMS 84

Impression III (Concert). 1911

Oil on canvas, 77.5 × 100 cm,
signed: Kandinsky 1911.
Inv. No. GMS 78

Impression IV (Torchlight Procession). 1911

Oil on canvas, 95 × 107 cm,
signed (on the back): Kandinsky.
Inv. No. GMS 85

Improvisation 21a. 1911

Oil on canvas, 96 × 105 cm,
signed: Kandinsky 1911.
Inv. No. GMS 82

St. George I. 1911

Oil on canvas, 97.5 × 107.5 cm,
signed: Kandinsky 1911.
Inv. No. GMS 81

All Saints II. 1911

Oil on canvas, 86 × 99 cm.
Inv. No. GMS 62

St. Vladimir. 1911

Painting on glass, 29 × 25.6 cm,
signed (on the back): Kandinsky / Gemalt im Juni
1911 in Murnau.
Frame painted by Kandinsky.
Inv. No. GMS 127

St. George I. 1911

Painting on glass, 19 × 19.7 cm,
signed (on the back): Kandinsky / Gemalt im Juni
1911 in Murnau.
Frame painted by Kandinsky.
Inv. No. GMS 105

St. George II. About 1911

Painting on glass, 29.8 × 14.7 cm.
Frame painted by Kandinsky.
Inv. No. GMS 110

All Saints I. 1911

Painting on glass, 34.5 × 40.5 cm.
Frame painted by Kandinsky.
Inv. No. GMS 107

Hell-hound and Bird of Paradise. 1911

Painting on glass, 10.8 × 9.2 cm,
signed (on the back): Kandinsky / Juni 1911
Murnau.
Inv. No. GMS 116

Angel of the Last Judgment. 1911

Painting on glass, (fragment), 26 × 17 cm,
signed (on the back): Kandinsky / Gemalt im
August 1911 in Murnau.
Frame painted by Kandinsky.
Inv. No. GMS 113

Resurrection. 1911

Painting on glass, 21.7 × 11.6 cm,
signed (on the back): Kandinsky / Gemalt im
August 1911 in Murnau.
Frame painted by Kandinsky.
Inv. No. GMS 112

Large Resurrection. About 1911

Painting on glass, 23.8 × 24 cm,
signed with monogram.
Frame painted by Kandinsky.
Inv. No. GMS 125

St. Gabriel. About 1911

Painting on glass, 40 × 25.3 cm.
Inv. No. GMS 123

Horsemen of the Apocalypse I. 1911

Painting on glass, 29.5 × 20.3 cm.
Frame painted by Kandinsky.
Inv. No. GMS 121

All Saints II. About 1911

Painting on glass, 31.3 × 48 cm,
signed with monogram.
Frame painted by Kandinsky.
Inv. No. GMS 122

Improvisation 26 (Oars). 1912

Oil on canvas, 97 × 107.5 cm,
signed: Kandinsky 1912.
Inv. No. GMS 66
Plate 30

A Cow in Moscow. 1912

Painting on glass, 28 × 32.2 cm,
signed with monogram.
Frame painted by Kandinsky.
Inv. No. 109

Painting on glass with Swan. About 1912

(The Announcement of the "Blue Rider").
Painting on glass, 32 × 27.7 cm,
signed with monogram.
Frame painted by Kandinsky.
Inv. No. GMS 118

Rowing. About 1912

Painting on glass, 22 × 26 cm.
Frame painted by Kandinsky.
Inv. No. GMS 108

Boat. About 1912

Tempera on paper, 26.2 × 26.7 cm,
signed with monogram.
Inv. No. GMS 615

A Lady in Moscow. About 1912

Oil on canvas, 108.8 × 108.8 cm,
signed (on the back): Kandinsky
Inv. No. GMS 73

A Lady in Moscow. About 1912

Painting on glass, 33.2 × 30.6 cm,
signed with monogram.
Frame painted by Kandinsky.
Inv. No. GMS 124

Small Pleasures. About 1912

Painting on glass, 30.6 × 40.3 cm.
Frame painted by Kandinsky.
Inv. No. GMS 120

Cavalier. About 1912

Painting on glass, 30.5 × 19.9 cm,
signed with monogram.
Frame painted by Kandinsky.
Inv. No. GMS 128

Improvisation (the Flood). 1913
(Study for *Composition VI*)

Oil on canvas, 95 × 150 cm.
Inv. No. GMS 76
Plate 31

Sketch for Improvisation 30 (Canons). 1913

Tempera on paper, 52.5 × 52.5 cm,
signed with monogram.
Inv. No. GMS 584

Study for Composition VII. 1913

Oil on canvas, 78 × 99.5 cm,
signed (on the back): Kandinsky — Studie
(zu Komposition 7) 1913, No. 183.
Inv. No. GMS 63

Study for Composition VII (Sketch 2). 1913

Oil on canvas, 100 × 140 cm,
signed (on the back): Kandinsky — zu Kompo-
position 7 (Entwurf 2) 1913, No. 182.
Inv. No. GMS 64

Study for Composition VII (Sketch 3). 1913

Oil on canvas, 89.5 × 125 cm,
signed (on the back): Kandinsky — zu Komposition 7 (Entwurf 3) 1913, No. 185
Inv. No. GMS 68

With red Spot. About 1913

Painting on glass, 27.2 × 24.4 cm,
signed with monogram.
Inv. No. GMS 126

St. George III. About 1913

Painting on glass, 23.8 × 23.5 cm.
Inv. No. GMS 119

Red Spot [Nächtlich]. 1913–14

Oil on canvas, 100 × 88 cm,
signed (on the back): Kandinsky 1913–14.
Inv. No. GMS 80

Untitled Painting (the Flood). 1914

Mixed media on canvas, 108×139.5 cm.
Inv. No. GMS 72

Large study for the summer panel for Mr. Campbell's apartment in New York. 1914

Oil on canvas, 99×59.5 cm.
Inv. No. GMS 75
Plate 34

Small study for the summer panel for Mr. Campbell's apartment in New York. 1914

Oil on cardboard, 64.5×49.5 cm,
signed with monogram.
Inv. No. GMS 65

Small study for the autumn panel for Mr. Campbell's apartment in New York. 1914

Oil on cardboard, 64.5×50 cm,
signed with monogram.
Inv. No. GMS 67

Small study for the winter panel for Mr. Campbell's apartment in New York. 1914

Oil on cardboard, 64×50.2 cm.
Inv. No. GMS 70

Improvisation (Gorge). 1914

Oil on canvas, 110×110 cm.
Inv. No. GMS 74
Plate 33

Untitled Improvisation. 1914

Oil on canvas, 124.5×73.5 cm.
Inv. No. GMS 69
Plate 35

Horsemen of the Apocalypse II. 1914

Painting on glass, 30×21.3 cm.
Inv. No. GMS 106
Plate 32

Sketch for the Horsemen of the Apocalypse II. 1914

Painting on glass, 13×9.8 cm.
Inv. No. GMS 115

Alexander Kanoldt

Born 29 September 1881 in Karlsruhe, died 24 January 1939 in Berlin. In 1899–1901 he studied under his father at the School for Arts and Crafts and 1901–4 at the Academy in Karlsruhe. In 1909 he was co-founder and secretary of the NKVM, and in 1913 joined the *Münchener Neue Sezession.* He withdrew in 1920 and became friends with Schrimpf and Mense. He was one of the most prominent artists of the *Neue Sachlichkeit.* From 1923 he was at the Berlin Academy, and was professor for a year (1925) at the Academy in Breslau.

Still Life of Cactus Flower. 1923

Oil on canvas, 100×70 cm, signed (on the back): Kanoldt, Stilleben VII/1923.
From the collection of his friend Erbslöh.
Inv. No. G 14222

Paul Klee

Born 18 December 1879 in Münchenbuchsee, near Berne, died 29 June 1940 in Muralto, near Locarno. His father was a musician from Bavaria; his mother came from Basle. As a child, Klee played the violin in the Berne orchestra. Having decided to become a painter, he went to Munich in 1898, attended L. Knirr's private school and in 1900 studied with Stuck at the Academy. He traveled in Italy in 1901 and spent 1902–6 in Berne. In 1906 he moved to Munich, where he became friends with Kubin. In 1911 he met the members of the NKVM, including Kandinsky and Marc. In 1912 he went to Paris and met Delaunay, whose essay, "De la lumière," he translated into German. Seventeen of his drawings were included in the second "Blue Rider" exhibition, and in 1913 he became a member of the *Münchener Neue Sezession.* In April 1914 he traveled to Tunis with Macke and Moilliet. He spent 1916–18 in military service. In 1921 Gropius invited him to join the Bauhaus staff. In 1924, with Kandinsky, Jawlensky, and Feininger, he became a member of the "Blue Four." The next year he participated in the first Surrealist exhibition in Paris. In 1929 he traveled to Egypt. The following year he was invited by Kaesbach to

accept a professorship at the Academy in Düsseldorf. In 1933, having been dismissed by the Nazis,
he moved to Berne.

Near Boll, at the foot of the Dentenberg. 1897

Pen on paper, 14.5 × 19.5 cm,
signed: PK. (intertwined) VII. 97.
From the estate of his sister Mathilde.
Inv. No. G 13022

Virgin in a Tree. 1903

Etching, 23.8 × 29.6 cm.
Donated by Gabriele Münter.
Inv. No. G 13113
Plate 36

*Meeting of two men, each suspecting the other to
be in a superior position.* 1903

Etching, 31.8 × 11 cm.
From Gabriele Münter's collection.
Inv. No. GMS 715

Female Nude. About 1904

Oil on cardboard, 28 × 23.4 cm.
From the Max Huggler Collection, Berne.
Inv. No. G 13001

The Hero with the Wing. 1905

Etching, 41.8 × 32.1 cm, inscribed: Für Lilly.
From Gabriele Münter's collection.
Inv. No. GMS 686

Senile Phoenix. 1905

Etching, 41.9 × 31.1 cm.
From Gabriele Münter's collection.
Inv. No. GMS 685

Still Life with Cacti. About 1906

Oil on cardboard, 52 × 41.5 cm.
Inv. No. G 12840
Plate 37

Two Statues. 1908

Painting on glass, 12.9 × 17.8 cm,
signed: Klee 1908.
Donated by Gabriele Münter.
Inv. No. G 13114
Plate 38

Boy in a fur-collared Coat. 1909

Watercolor, 22.5 × 31.5 cm. On the back: Interieur
mit Petroleumlampe; signed: 1909.65. Klee.
Donated by Gabriele Münter.
Inv. No. G 13115
Plate 39

Corner of a Garden. 1910

Watercolor, 13.9 × 13.3 cm, signed: Klee 1910. 47
Donated by Gabriele Münter.
Inv. No. G 13116
Plate 41

Oberwiesenfeld. 1910

Painting on glass, 23 × 29 cm, signed: Klee 1910. 59.
Inv. No. G 13265

Railroad Station. 1911

Drypoint, 14.8 × 19.8 cm, signed (in the plate):
1911. 26; (on the print): Bahnhof. Klee.
Inv. No. G 13483

Four Figurines at two Tables. 1912

Pen on paper, 6.8 × 10.5 cm, signed: Klee. 1912. 28.
Donated by Gabriele Münter.
Inv. No. G 13117

Female Dancer. 1912

Pen on paper, 8.8 × 6.2 cm, signed: Klee. 1912. 29.
Donated by Gabriele Münter.
Inv. No. 13118
Plate 40

Street Arabs [Gassenkinder]. 1912

Lithograph, 8.9 × 12.7 cm, signed: Klee. 1912. 118.
From Gabriele Münter's collection.
Inv. No. GMS 687

Crossroads. 1913

Watercolor, 13.7 × 26.6 cm, signed: Klee 1913. 27.
Donated by Gabriele Münter.
Inv. No. G 13119
Plate 43

Suburb (Munich North). 1913

Mixed media, 12.1 × 19.4 cm,
signed: Klee 1913. 199.
Donated by Gabriele Münter.
Inv. No. G 13120
Plate 44

Miraculous Draught of Fishes. 1913

Pen on paper, 17 × 5.8/7.4 cm,
signed: Klee 1913. 126.
From Gabriele Münter's collection.
Inv. No. GMS 689.
Plate 42

The Battlefield. 1913

Gouache, 11.6 × 20.7 cm, signed: Klee.
On permanent loan from the Gabriele Münter and
Johannes Eichner Foundation

Postcard with a drawing, to Gabriele Münter. 1913

Pen on paper, 6.6 × 5.1 cm (glued to postcard).
From Gabriele Münter's collection.
Inv. No. GMS 725

Sacred Stones and Idols. 1913

Pen on paper, 5.3 × 16.4 cm,
signed: Klee 1913. 141.
From Gabriele Münter's collection.
Inv. No. GMS 690

Garden of Passion. 1913.

Etching, 25.9 × 36.8 cm, signed: Klee. 1913. 155.
From Gabriele Münter's collection.
Inv. No. GMS 688

Drawing with Trumpeter. About 1914

Pen on paper, 17.1 × 10.4 cm.
From Gabriele Münter's collection.
Inv. No. GMS 691

Drawing with roman numerals. About 1914

Pen on paper, 22.4 × 11.5 cm.
From Gabriele Münter's collection.
Inv. No. GMS 692

Drawing with male Figure. About 1914

Pen on paper, 11.7 × 11.7 cm.
From Gabriele Münter's collection.
Inv. No. GMS 693

Drawing. About 1914

Pen on paper, 12.9 × 7.1 cm.
From Gabriele Münter's collection.
Inv. No. GMS 694

Microcosm. 1914

Etching, 14.4 × 9.6 cm,
signed (in the plate): 1914/120 Kl.; (on the print:
Kleinwelt / für Madelaine Weihnachten 1914 /
Klee.
Inv. No. G 13471

South wind [Föhn] in Marc's Garden. 1915

Watercolor, 20 × 15 cm, signed: Klee 1915. 102.
Inv. No. G 13266
Plate 45

Castles in the Air. 1915

Etching, 18.5 × 26.8 cm, signed: Klee 1915. 212.
Donated by Gabriele Münter.
Inv. No. G 13121

Destruction and Hope. 1916

Lithograph, colored, 52.5 × 39.8 cm,
signed: Klee, Zerstörung und Hoffnung.
Donated by Gabriele Münter.
Inv. No. G 13122

Town R. 1919

Mixed media on gesso, 16.5 × 22 cm,
signed: Klee 1919. 205.
On permanent loan from the Gabriele Münter and
Johannes Eichner Foundation.
Plate 46

A Comedy with Birds [Vogelkomödie]. 1919

Lithograph, 50.8 × 36.5 cm, signed: Klee.
Donated by Gabriele Münter.
Inv. No. G 13123

Five Lithographs

28×23 cm, published in: *Münchner Blätter für Dichtung und Graphik*, Vol. I, 1919.
Inv. No. G 13155

a) *Three Heads.* Signed: Klee 1919.9.
3rd issue, p. 38

b) *Acrobats.* Signed: 1919.10.
1st issue, p. 10

c) *"Zahlenbaum Landschaft."*
Signed: Klee 1919, 112
9th issue, p. 142

d) *Meditation, self-portrait.*
Signed: Klee 1919. 113
9th issue, p. 143

e) *The horrible Dream.* Signed: K. 1919.212.
11th/12th issue, p. 185

The giant Plant Louse [Die Riesenblattlaus]. 1920
1920

Lithograph, 32.3×23.6 cm.
Donated by Gabriele Münter.
Inv. No. G 13124

Ten Lithographs (reproduced drawings) in Kurt Corrinth, *Potsdamer Platz.*
Georg Müller Verlag, Munich, 1920.
Lib. Cat. No. 1860

The wild Man. 1922

Mixed media on gesso, 58.6×38.8 cm,
signed: S. Cl. Klee.
On permanent loan from the Gabriele Münter and Johannes Eichner Foundation.
Plate 47

Archangel. 1938

Oil on canvas, 100×65 cm, signed: Klee.
On permanent loan from the Gabriele Münter and Johannes Eichner Foundation.
Plate 48

Moissej Kogan

Born 24 (12) May 1879 in Orgejev, Bessarabia, died 1938 in Paris. He lived in Munich from 1903 to 1910. Mostly self-taught, he studied for a short time with the sculptor W. Rümann. He worked during this period as lapidary, medallist, potter, and designer for embroidery and weaving patterns. He spent some time with H. van de Velde in Weimar and at the Folkwang Museum, Essen, before going to Paris in 1910. He became friends with Rodin and Maillol. He participated in the three NKVM exhibitions. He lived from time to time in Ascona and was in Holland in 1924, 1928, and 1933.

Neue Künstlervereinigung München medal. 1910

Bronze, diameter: 2.9 cm.
From Gabriele Münter's collection.
Inv. No. GMS 695

Medal with three female figures. About 1910.

Bronze, diameter: 5.3 cm.
From Gabriele Münter's collection.
Inv. No. GMS 696

Medal with two female nudes. About 1910

Silver, 2.4×1.8 cm (oval).
From Gabriele Münter's collection.
Inv. No. GMS 697

Seated Nude. About 1910 (?)

Woodcut, 41×31 cm, signed: M. Kogan.
Donated by Gabriele Münter.
Inv. No. G 13125

Dancer. About 1910 (?)

Linocut, 42.1×24.1 cm, signed: M. Kogan.
Donated by Gabriele Münter.
Inv. No. G 13127

Two Dancers. About 1910 (?)

Linocut, 35.5×27.8 cm, signed: M. Kogan.
Donated by Gabriele Münter.
Inv. No. G 13126

Dance before the Temple. About 1910 (?)

Drypoint, 35.7 × 25.1 cm, signed: M. Kogan.
Donated by Gabriele Münter.
Inv. No. 13129

Daphnis and Chloe. About 1910 (?)

Drypoint, 37.2 × 27 cm, signed: M. Kogan.
Inv. No. G 13128

Girl with Flower. About 1910 (?)

Linocut, 25 × 11.9 cm.
Inv. No. G 12845

Female Head. About 1910

Wool embroidery, 16.7 × 17.7 cm.
Donated by Clotilde von Derp-Sacharov, Rome.
Inv. No. G 13345

Relief in three parts. 1924

Bronze

a) one male and one female nude, 16 × 9 cm.
b) three female nudes, 16 × 11 cm.
c) two female nudes, 16 × 9 cm.

Inv. No. G 12782

Alfred Kubin

Born 10 April 1877 in Leitmeritz, Bohemia, died
20 August 1959 in Zwickledt, near Wernstein am
Inn, Austria. Moved to Munich in 1898, studied
the Old Masters, and spent a brief period at the
Munich Academy. A resident in Zwickledt from
1906, he traveled to Dalmatia in 1907 and to the
Balkans in 1909. He became a member of the NKVM
in 1909 and participated in its first and second
exhibitions. He withdrew from the NKVM in 1911
with Kandinsky, Marc, and Münter. Eleven of his
pen drawings were included in the second "Blue
Rider" exhibition.

Man kneeling before a naked Woman. About 1902

Mixed media, 20.4 × 24.3 cm,
signed: AK (intertwined).
Donated by Gabriele Münter.
Inv. No. G 13130

Intruders. 1904

Pen and Indian ink on paper, 19.7 × 28.4 cm.
From Gabriele Münter's collection.
Inv. No. GMS 699

Deep Sea. 1906

Gouache, 35.5 × 35 cm.
Inv. No. G 12416

Thunderstorm. 1906

Gouache, 32 × 35 cm, signed: Kubin.
Inv. No. G 12415
Plate 49

The Christ Thistle. About 1907

Pencil on paper, 19.5 × 24.1 cm.
From Gabriele Münter's collection.
Inv. No. GMS 703

Illustration for Hauff's Fairy Tales. 1908

Pen and Indian ink on paper, 11 × 18.2 cm,
signed: Kubin.
Inv. No. G 9007

Aurelie. Before 1910

Pen and Indian ink on paper, 31.2 × 19.8 cm,
signed: Kubin.
Donated by Gabriele Münter.
Inv. No. G 13132

Meeting in the Snow. About 1910–12

Pen and Indian ink on paper, 28.3 × 18.3 cm,
inscribed: Meinem lieben Kandinsky und dem ver-
ehrten Fräulein Münter / Alfred Kubin.
From Gabriele Münter's collection.
Inv. No. GMS 700

The Fugitive. 1912

Lithograph, 22 × 27.5 cm, signed: Kubin.
Inv. No. G 1604

The Spirit of the Air. 1912

Pen and Indian ink on paper, 20 × 31.5 cm,
signed: July 1912 / Kubin für Fräulein Münter.
From Gabriele Münter's collection.
Inv. No. GMS 701

Female Nude on Bed. About 1912

Indian ink on paper, 19.7 × 31.1 cm, signed: Kubin.
From Gabriele Münter's collection.
Inv. No. GMS 702

In the Jungle. About 1913

Pen and Indian ink on paper, 31,6 × 39.1 cm,
inscribed: S. [einem] lieben Kandinsky mit herz-
lichem Glückwunsch / Kubin.
From Gabriele Münter's collection.
Inv. No. GMS 713
Plate 50

The deserted City. 1916

Lithograph, 24.6 × 19.7 cm, signed: Kubin.
Inv. No. G 1610

Der Elementargeist. Before 1920

Watercolor, 31.7 × 39.6 cm, signed: Kubin.
Donated by Gabriele Münter.
Inv. No. G 13133

The Escape. 1920

Lithograph, 18.5 × 25.5 cm, signed: Kubin.
Inv. No. G 1603

Wolfgang Gurlitt in his Berlin home. About 1920

Lithograph, 32.4 × 24.4 cm, signed: AK (joined).
Donated by Wolfgang Gurlitt, Munich.
Inv. No. G 12188

Fairy-tale Forest. About 1920

Pen and Indian ink on paper, 27.7 × 25.7 cm,
signed: Alf. Kubin.
From Gabriele Münter's collection.
Inv. No. GMS 722

The Werwolf. 1912

Lithograph, 24 × 19 cm, signed: A. Kubin.
Inv. No. G 1611

The mangy Cat. 1922

Lithograph, 17 × 23.5 cm,
signed: Kubin, Die räudige Katze.
Inv. No. G 1606

The enchanted Prince. 1923

Pen on paper, 35.4 × 26.1 cm,
signed: A. Kubin (joined).
Donated by Gabriele Münter.
Inv. No. G 13134
Plate 51

Death in a Tree. 1923

Lithograph, 26.5 × 35.5 cm, signed: Kubin.
Inv. No. G 1609

The Face of the Tiger. 1923

Lithograph, 20 × 33 cm, signed: A. Kubin.
Inv. No. G 1601

New World. 1923

(Illustration to a poem by Hölderlin).
Lithograph, 44 × 33 cm, signed: Kubin.
Inv. No. G 1605

Pietà. 1923

Lithograph, 44 × 31.5 cm, signed: Kubin.
Inv. No. G 12150

Riviera. 1924

Lithograph, 13.6 × 26.3 cm, signed: Kubin.
Inv. No. G 1607

The Man of Sorrows (Christ wearing the Robe). 1924

Lithograph, 35 × 24 cm, signed: Kubin.
Inv. No. G 1608

Hunter and Nymph. About 1924

Pen and Indian ink on paper, 19.7 × 31.2 cm,
signed: Kubin.
From Gabriele Münter's collection.
Inv. No. GMS 698

Stallion and Snake. 1924

Lithograph, 23.3 × 25.5 cm, signed Kubin.
Inv. No. G 1612

End of the Carnival. 1925

Lithograph, 20 × 33 cm, signed: Kubin.
Inv. No. G 1602

The Brooder. 1926

Lithograph, 43.5 × 34.2 cm, signed: Kubin.
Inv. No. G 2134

Autumn. Before 1927

Pen and Indian ink on paper, 9.1 × 15.6 cm,
signed: A. Kubin.
Donated by the artist.
Inv. No. G 822

Carrier's Cart (Bolting Team). Before 1927

Pen and Indian ink on paper, 24.1 × 31.5 cm,
signed: A. Kubin.
Inv. No. G 690

Giant Snakes. 1928

Pen on paper, 39.5 × 31 cm, signed: A. Kubin / 28.
Inv. No. G 1990

From Wernstein (Encounter). 1928

Pen and Indian ink on paper, 38.6 × 31.5 cm,
signed: A. Kubin (joined) / 28.
From Gabriele Münter's collection.
Inv. No. GMS 704

Infamous Place. About 1928

Pen and Indian ink on paper, 31.3 × 38.5 cm,
signed: A. Kubin.
Inv. No. G 2356

The three Fates. 1929

Lithograph, 31 × 41 cm, signed: Kubin.
Inv. No. G 1991

Transport in the Mountains. About 1929

Lithograph, 40.8 × 31 cm, signed: A. Kubin.
Inv. No. 1992

Demosthenes. About 1929

Pen and Indian ink on paper, 25.8 × 17.3 cm,
signed: A. Kubin.
Inv. No. G 1600

Plaintive Song. About 1930

Pen and Indian ink on paper, 35.5 × 26.5 cm,
signed: A. Kubin.
Inv. No. G 2358

Orpheus. About 1930

Pen on paper, 41 × 31.5 cm,
signed: A. Kubin (joined).
Inv. No. G 2354

The Hobbyhorse. About 1930 (?)

Pen with watercolor on paper, 40 × 31.5 cm,
signed: A. Kubin.
Inv. No. G 2355

The rigid Woman [Die Erstarrte]. About 1930

Pen with wash on paper, 42 × 31.8 cm,
signed: Kubin.
Inv. No. G 2357

The Lion's Gorge. 1931

Lithograph, 30 × 25 cm, signed: Kubin
Inv. No. G 2785

The Erl-king's Daughters. 1932

Lithograph, 30.5 × 24.5 cm,
signed: A. Kubin (joined).
Inv. No. G 2783

Tiger Hunt. 1932

Lithograph, 31 × 29.5 cm, signed: A. Kubin.
Inv. No. G 2784

Rübezahl II. 1944

Lithograph, 54 × 36 cm, signed: Kubin.
Donated by Günther Franke, Munich.
Inv. No. G 12723

Else Lasker-Schüler

Born 11 February 1876 in Elberfeld, Germany,
died 22 January 1945 in Jerusalem. A writer and
painter, she illustrated a large number of her own
books. She was a friend of Franz Marc, who called
her "Prince Jusuff." She emigrated to Israel in
1933.

Ten illustrations for her poem "Prince Jusuff."
Lithographs, hand-colored, all 32 × 23 cm, signed:
Else Lasker-Schüler.
Inv. No. G 12563 a–k

August Macke

Born 3 January 1887 in Meschede on the Ruhr, died
in action 26 September 1914 near Perthes, Cham-
pagne. He studied in 1904–5 at the Academy and
later with Ehmcke at the School for Arts and Crafts
in Düsseldorf. In 1907 he first visited Paris, with
his future wife's uncle, Bernhard Koehler. The winter of 1907 he spent with Lovis Corinth in Berlin.
In 1908 he made a second visit to Paris and spent
1909–10 in Tegernsee. He became friends with
Marc. He was a contributor to the *Almanach Der
Blaue Reiter.* Three of his paintings were included
in the first "Blue Rider" exhibition, and four works
(material unspecified) as well as twelve drawings in
the second. In 1912 he was in Bonn. He participated in the *Sonderbund* exhibition in Cologne.
With Marc he visited Delaunay in Paris in September 1912. He spent eight months in 1913 in Hilterfingen on the Lake of Thun, Switzerland. In 1914
he traveled to Tunis with Klee and Moilliet. In
August of that year he was drafted.

Fishermen on the Rhine. 1907

Oil on cardboard, 40.3 × 44.5 cm,
signed: Aug. Macke 07.
Bernhard Koehler Bequest, 1965.
Inv. No. G 13330
Plate 52

Portrait of Bernhard Koehler, Sr. 1908

Oil on canvas, 36.5 × 31.5 cm.
Inv. No. G 12295

Study for "Portrait with Apples." 1909

Oil on wood, 38.5 × 31.5 cm.
On loan from Joseph Staudacher, Tegernsee

Portrait with Apples. 1909

Oil on canvas, 66 × 59.5 cm,
signed: A. Macke, 1909.
Bernhard Koehler Bequest, 1965.
Inv. No. G 13326
Plate 53

Self-portrait. 1909–10

Oil on cardboard, 34.5 × 26 cm.
On loan from Joseph Staudacher, Tegernsee

A Corner of the Living Room in Tegernsee. 1910

Oil on canvas, 42 × 48 cm, signed: A. Macke, 1910.
Donated by Bernhard Koehler, 1962.
Inv. No. G 13024
Plate 54

Portrait of Bernhard Koehler, Sr. 1910

Oil on canvas, 63.5 × 41 cm.
Bernhard Koehler Bequest, 1965.
Inv. No. G 13335
Plate 55

Flowers on the Windowsill. 1910

Oil on canvas, 62 × 39 cm.
Formerly in the Bernhard Koehler Collection,
Berlin.
Inv. No. G 13065
Plate 56

Farmboy from Tegernsee. 1910

Oil on canvas, 88 × 66.5 cm.
Inv. No. G 12195
Plate 57

Japanese Roses in a blue Glass. 1910

Oil on canvas, 65.2 × 43.5 cm.
Donated by Gabriele Münter.
Inv. No. G 13135

Three Nudes with blue Background. 1910

Oil on canvas, 72 × 59 cm, signed: Macke, 1910.
On permanent loan from the Gabriele Münter and
Johannes Eichner Foundation

Morning over the Tegernsee. 1910

Oil on cardboard, 34.5 × 54 cm.
Inv. No. G 13902

Mounted Red Indians. 1911

Oil on wood, 44 × 60 cm.
Bernhard Koehler Bequest, 1965.
Inv. No. G 13327
Plate 58

Mounted Red Indians by a Tent. 1911

Oil on wood, 26.5 × 35.5 cm.
Inv. No. G 13261

River with Fisherman. About 1911

Painting on glass, 15.4 × 22 cm.
From Gabriele Münter's collection.
Inv. No. GMS 719

In the Circus. 1911

Painting on glass, 11.8 × 8.9 cm.
From Gabriele Münter's collection.
Inv. No. GMS 721

Two Girls in a Landscape. 1911

Painting on glass, 19.5 × 25.5 cm.
From Gabriele Münter's collection.
Inv. No. GMS 720

Three Girls in a Boat. 1911

Painting on glass, 37 × 56 cm.
Inv. No. G 12983

Maria and Franz Marc in Macke's Studio, Bonn.
1912

Pastel, 31.9 × 27.1 cm.
From Gabriele Münter's collection.
Inv. No. GMS 724

The Zoo I. 1912

Oil on canvas, 58.5 × 98 cm.
Bernhard Koehler Bequest, 1965.
Inv. No. G 13329
Plate 59

St. George. 1912

Brush and Indian ink on paper, 63.3 × 49.6 cm.
Donated by Gabriele Münter.
Inv. No. G 12557

The Bumpy Cab [Die rüttelnde Droschke]. 1912

Postcard from August and Elisabeth Macke, Franz
and Maria Marc, and Herwarth Walden, to Kan-
dinsky.
Pencil, 9.1 × 14.1 cm.
From Gabriele Münter's collection.
Inv. No. GMS 718

Salutation. 1912

Linocut, 24.3 × 19.6 cm.
Inv. No. G 12660

Carpet of Flowers. 1913

Oil on canvas, 60.5 × 48.5 cm,
signed: A. Macke, 1913.
Inv. No. G 12193
Plate 60

Promenade. 1913

Oil on cardboard, 51 × 57 cm,
signed: August Macke 1913
Bernhard Koehler Bequest, 1965.
Inv. No. G 13328
Plate 61

Our Street in Grey. 1913

Oil on canvas, 80 × 57.5 cm,
signed (on the back): Macke August 1913.
Bernhard Koehler Bequest, 1965.
Inv. No. G 13333
Plate 62

A Millinery Shop. 1913

Oil on canvas, 54.5 × 44 cm, signed: Macke 1913.
Bernhard Koehler Bequest, 1965.
Inv. No. G 13334
Plate 63

Promenade on a Bridge. 1913

Oil on cardbord, 24.7 × 30.2 cm.
Bernhard Koehler Bequest, 1965.
Inv. No. 13332
Plate 64

Children with a Goat. 1913

Oil on cardboard, 24 × 34 cm,
signed: Aug. Macke 1913.
Bernhard Koehler Bequest, 1965.
Inv. No. G 13331
Plate 65

Abstract Shapes II. 1913

Crayon on paper, 20.5 × 15.7 cm.
Inv. No. G 12403

Persiflage on the Blue Rider. 1913

Watercolor, 24.6 × 34.5 cm, signed: A. Macke 1913.
There are caricatures of the following persons:
Herwarth Walden, August Macke, Maria Marc,
Kandinsky, Gabriele Münter, and Franz Marc.
Donated by Gabriele Münter.
Inv. No. G 13137

Female Nude with Scarf. 1913

Pencil on paper, 31.8 × 27 cm.
Donated by Gabriele Münter.
Inv. No. G 13136

Turkish Café II. 1914

Oil on wood, 60 × 35 cm, signed: Aug. Macke 1914.
Bernhard Koehler Bequest, 1965.
Inv. No. G 13325
Plate 66

Garden Gate. 1914

Watercolor, 31 × 22.5 cm.
On permanent loan from the Gabriele Münter and
Johannes Eichner Foundation

Elisabeth Macke

Born 11 May 1888 in Bonn, lives there. She introduced August Macke to her uncle, Bernhard Koehler, Sr. On 9 September 1916 she married the writer Lothar Erdmann.

Woman with Child. 1911

Painting on glass, 9 × 12 cm.
Frame painted by Kandinsky.
From Gabriele Münter's collection.
On permanent loan from the Gabriele Münter and
Johannes Eichner Foundation

Franz Marc

Born 8 February 1880 in Munich, died in action 4 March 1916 at Verdun. After studying philosophy and theology at the university, he went to the Academy in Munich to learn painting with Hackl and Wilhelm von Diez. A visit to France in 1903 produced no immediate artistic results. He moved to Sindelsdorf, Upper Bavaria, in 1910, became friends with Macke, and met Bernhard Koehler. In

1911 he became a member of the NKVM, but withdrew in November. He and Kandinsky founded the "Blue Rider," organized two exhibitions, and published the *Almanach Der Blaue Reiter*. Four of his paintings were included in the first exhibition, and four drawings and one colored woodcut in the second. In 1912 he and Macke visited Delaunay in Paris. In 1913 he participated in the organization of the first German *Herbstsalon* in Berlin. He moved to Ried, near Benediktbeuren, in 1914.

Portrait of the Artist's Father. 1902

Oil on cardboard, 73 × 50.8 cm.
Inv. No. G 10672

Portrait of the Artist's Mother. 1902

Oil on canvas, 98.5 × 70 cm.
Inv. No. G 10671
Plate 67

Herdboy in a mountain Hut. 1902

Oil on canvas, 39 × 26.5 cm.
Donated by Maria Marc, 1955.
Inv. No. G 11799

A Cowherd. 1902

Oil on canvas, 30.5 × 40.5 cm,
signed: Staffelalm 02.
Donated by Maria Marc, 1955.
Inv. No. G 11798

Alpine Pasture II with Lambs. 1902

Oil on canvas, 28 × 44.5 cm,
signed: Staffelalm Sept. 02.
Donated by Maria Marc, 1955.
Inv. No. G 11797

Jumping Dog (Schlick). 1904

Oil on cardboard, 54.5 × 67.5 cm.
Formerly in the collection of Dr. Paul Marc,
the artist's brother.
Inv. No. G 11481
Plate 68

Portrait of a Painter. 1906
(Maria Marc painting in the snow)

Oil on canvas, 56.5 × 41 cm.
Formerly in the collection of Margarete Macke.
Donated by Gabriele Münter.
Inv. No. G 13138

Orpheus and the Animals. 1908

Design for a tapestry.
Oil on canvas, 74.5 × 134.5 cm, signed: Fz. M. 07.
Inv. No. G 13199
Plate 69

Landscape with Trees. 1908

Watercolor, 30.4 × 41.5 cm, signed: Fz. Marc 1908.
Inv. No. G 12388

Dying Deer. 1908

Lithograph, 19.3 × 20.8 cm, signed: Fz. M.
From Gabriele Münter's collection.
Inv. No. GMS 705

The Panther. 1908

Bronze, height: 9.8 cm.
On permanent loan from the Gabriele Münter and
Johannes Eichner Foundation.

Two Horses. 1908–9

Bronze, height: 16.4 cm,
monogrammed on the base.
Bernhard Koehler Bequest, 1965.
Inv. No. G 13319
Plate 70

Deer at Twilight. 1909

Oil on canvas, 70.5 × 100.5 cm, signed: Frz. Marc.
Formerly in the Bernhard Koehler Collection,
Berlin.
Donated by Gabriele Münter.
Inv. No. G 12763
Plate 71

Young Oak Tree. 1909

Oil on canvas, 83.5 × 104 cm, signed: Marc.
Donated by Gabriele Münter.
Inv. No. G 12765
Plate 72

Grazing Horses II (?). 1910

Oil on canvas, 64 × 94 cm.
Donated by the Bavarian Government on the
occasion of the 800th anniversary of the city of
Munich, 1958.
Inv. No. G 12576
Plate 74

Two Cats. 1910

Colored lithograph. Poster for the Marc exhibition
in Brakls Moderne Kunsthandlung, Munich;
printed by H. Eigner, Munich. 92 × 63.4 cm.
Inv. No. G 13370

Nude with Cat. 1910

Oil on canvas, 88 × 82 cm.
Previously in the Bernhard Koehler Collection,
Berlin.
Inv. No. G 12762
Plate 73

Blue Horse I. 1911

Oil on canvas, 112 × 84.5 cm.
Bernhard Koehler Bequest, 1965.
Inv. No. G 13324
Plate 75

Standing Horse. 1911

Pencil on paper, 18 × 11 cm.
Inv. No. G 13478

Portrait of Henri Rousseau. 1911

Painting on glass, 15.3 × 11.4 cm,
signed (on the back): Franz Marc fec.
From Gabriele Münter's collection.
Inv. No. GMS 723

Jumping Horse. 1912

Pencil and charcoal on paper, 17 × 10 cm.
Inv. No. G 13477

Cows (red, green, yellow). 1912

Oil on canvas, 62 × 87.5 cm, signed: Marc.
Donated by Gabriele Münter.
Inv. No. G 13140
Plate 76

Deer in the Forest II. 1912

Oil on canvas, 110 × 81 cm, signed: Marc.
Bernhard Koehler Bequest, 1965.
Inv. No. G 13321
Plate 77

Red and Blue Horses. 1912

Mixed media, 26.5 × 34 cm, signed: Fz. Marc.
From Gabriele Münter's collection.
Inv. No. GMS 706
Plate 78

A little Monkey and a Man. About 1912

Oil on canvas, 35.5 × 51.5 cm.
Fragment of the destroyed painting *Savages.*
Donated by Gabriele Münter.
Inv. No. G 13139

The Tiger. 1912

Oil on canvas, 111 × 111.5 cm,
signed (on the back): Fz. Marc/12.
Bernhard Koehler Bequest, 1965.
Inv. No. G 13320
Plate 79

Deer in a Monastery Garden. 1912

Oil on canvas, 75.5 × 101 cm, signed: Marc.
Bernhard Koehler Bequest, 1965.
Inv. No. G 13323
Plate 80

In the Rain. 1912

Oil on canvas, 81 × 105.5 cm.
Bernhard Koehler Bequest, 1965.
Inv. No. G 13322
Plate 81

New Year's Greeting. 1912

Postcard to Gabriele Münter.
Pen and ink on paper, 9.5 × 14.4 cm.
From Gabriele Münter's collection.
Inv. No. GMS 716

Tiger. 1912

Woodcut, 30.4 × 32.8 cm, signed: M.
From Gabriele Münter's collection.
Inv. No. GMS 707

Animal Legend [Tierlegende]. 1912

Woodcut, 20 × 24 cm, signed: M.
From Gabriele Münter's collection.
Inv. No. GMS 710

Reconciliation. 1912

Woodcut, 24.7 × 33.9 cm, signed: M.
From Gabriele Münter's collection.
Inv. No. GMS 709

Drinking Horse. 1912

Woodcut, 36 × 21.3 cm, signed: M.
From Gabriele Münter's collection.
Inv. No. GMS 808

Wild Pony. 1912

Woodcut, 6.2 × 8 cm (on a postcard from Franz
Marc to Kandinsky), signed: M.
From Gabriele Münter's collection.
Inv. No. GMS 717

The Bull. 1912

Woodcut, 23.1 × 37.4 cm, signed: M.
Donated by Gabriele Münter.
Inv. No. G 13142

Legendary Animal [Fabeltier]. 1912

Colored woodcut, 18.3 × 25 cm, signed: Frz. Marc.
Published in the museum (de luxe) edition of the
Almanach Der Blaue Reiter, Munich, 1912.
Donated by Gabriele Münter.
Inv. No. G 13141

Four Foxes. 1913

Postcard to Kandinsky from Sindelsdorf,
4 February 1913.
Watercolor, 14 × 9 cm.
Inv. No. GMS 746

Two Animals. 1913

Postcard to Kandinsky from Sindelsdorf,
15 February 1913.
Watercolor, 9 × 14 cm.
Inv. No. GMS 747

Red and Blue Horses. 1913

Postcard to Kandinsky from Sindelsdorf,
5 April 1913.
Watercolor, 9 × 14 cm.
Inv. No. GMS 743

Vermilion Greeting [Zinnobergruß]. 1913

Postcard to Kandinsky from Sindelsdorf,
19 April 1913.
Watercolor, 14 × 9 cm.
Inv. No. GMS 726

The Lamb from an Altar in Lana. 1913

Postcard to Gabriele Münter from Sindelsdorf,
11 April 1913.
Watercolor, 9 × 14 cm.
Inv. No. GMS 741

Two Sheep. 1913

Postcard to Kandinsky from Sindelsdorf,
2 May 1913.
Watercolor and collage, 9 × 14 cm.
Inv. No. GMS 745

Two blue Horses in front of a red Rock. 1913

Postcard to Kandinsky from Sindelsdorf,
21 May 1913.
Tempera, 14 × 9 cm.
Inv. No. GMS 742

Byzantine Saint. 1913

Postcard to Kandinsky "sans barbe"
from Sindelsdorf, 8 June 1913.
Tempera, 14 × 9 cm.
Inv. No. GMS 744

Lion Hunt after Delacroix. 1913

Woodcut, 24 × 27 cm.
Inv. No. G 12698

Jumping Ponies. 1913

Woodcut, 13.5 × 9 cm.
One print on light-blue paper, signed: M.
Inv. No. G 1919
One print on white paper.
Donated by Gabriele Münter.
Inv. No. G 13143

Horse and Hedgehog. 1913

Woodcut, 23.1 × 28.3 cm, signed: M.
Donated by Gabriele Münter.
Inv. No. G 12716

The Birth of Horses. 1913

Colored woodcut, 21.5 × 14.5 cm, signed: M.
Donated by Gabriele Münter.
Inv. No. G 12717

Cock, Goat, and Pig. About 1914

Embroidery by Ada Campendonk from a design
by Franz Marc. Diameter: 22 cm.
Donated by Gabriele Münter.
Inv. No. G 13102

Stella Peregrina. 1917

18 facsimile reproductions of originals by Franz
Marc, hand-colored by Annette von Eckardt,
Verlag F. Hanfstaengl, Munich, 1917.
Inv. No. 12768

Gabriele Münter

Born 19 February 1877 in Berlin, died 19 May
1962 in Murnau. She spent her early youth in
Westphalia and Coblenz. She visited relatives in
the United States in 1898–1900. In 1901–2 she
studied with Angelo Jank at the *Künstlerinnen-
verein*, Munich. In 1902 she was at the "Phalanx"
school, first with Hüsgen in the sculpture class and
then with Kandinsky. She spent 1904–8 traveling
with Kandinsky. In September 1908 she and Kandinsky moved into an apartment at 36 Ainmillerstrasse, Munich, and in 1909 they bought a house

in Murnau, Upper Bavaria. She was a co-founder
of the NKVM in 1909, but withdrew with Kandinsky, Marc, and Kubin in November 1911. Six
of her paintings were included in the first "Blue
Rider" exhibition and fourteen works in the second. In 1913 she took part in the first German
Herbstsalon in Berlin. In 1914 she went to Switzerland with Kandinsky. In December 1915 she met
Kandinsky in Stockholm, but after Kandinsky's return to Moscow in the spring of 1916 they separated. In 1917–20 she was in Copenhagen, and
during the next seven years she visited Cologne,
Berlin, Ticino, and the Engadin. In 1929–30 she
was in France. From 1931 on she lived in Murnau
with few interruptions.

Kandinsky painting. 1903

Oil on canvas board, 16.9 × 25 cm,
signed (on the back): Gabriele Münter, Kandinsky
b. Landschaftsmalen, Kallmünz 1903.
Inv. No. GMS 649
Plate 82

Kallmünz. 1903

Oil on canvas, 26 × 17.3 cm,
signed (on the back): Kallmünz 1903.
Inv. No. GMS 650

Alley in the Parc de Saint-Cloud. 1906

Oil on canvas, 40.5 × 50.5 cm,
signed: G. Münter 1906.
Inv. No. GMS 651

View from a Window in Sèvres. 1906

Oil on canvas, 38 × 46 cm, signed: Münter.
Inv. No. G 11770
Plate 83

Landscape near Rapallo. 1906

Oil on canvas, 25.3 × 17.2 cm.
Inv. No. GMS 781

Trees in Blossom in Lana. 1908

Oil on canvas board, 17.7 × 25.7 cm.
Inv. No. GMS 647
Plate 84

Apples and Narcissi. 1908

Oil on cardboard, 66,5 × 49.7 cm,
signed (on the back): G. Münter.
Inv. No. GMS 653

View of the Murnau Marsh. 1908

Oil on cardboard, 32.7 × 40.5 cm,
signed: Mü (intertwined) 08; (on the back): Münter
1908, Blick aufs Moos.
Inv. No. GMS 654
Plate 85

St. Theresa. About 1908–9

(copy, probably after Rambold)
Painting on glass, 19 × 16.3 cm.
Inv. No. GMS 730

Votive. About 1908–9

(copy after Rambold).
Painting on glass, 19.5 × 13.2 cm.
Inv. No. GMS 731

St. Mary. About 1908–9

(copy after Rambold)
Painting on glass, 20 × 15 cm.
Inv. No. GMS 732

Portrait of Marianne von Werefkin. 1909

Oil on cardboard, 81 × 55 cm, signed: Münter.
Inv. No. GMS 656
Plate 86

Jawlensky and Werefkin. About 1908–9

Oil on cardboard, 32.7 × 44.5 cm.
Inv. No. GMS 655
Plate 87

Listening (portrait of Jawlensky). 1909

Oil on cardboard, 49.7 × 66.2 cm, signed: Münter.
Inv. No. GMS 657

Crosses in the Cemetery in Kochel. 1909

Oil on cardboard, 40.5 × 32.8 cm,
signed: Mü (intertwined).
Inv. No. GMS 658

Madonna with Child. About 1909–10

Painting on glass, 22.5 × 15.7 cm,
signed (on the back): Münter 1909 oder 10.
Frame painted by Kandinsky.
Inv. No. GMS 734

Autumnal. 1910

Oil on cardboard, 32.8 × 40.6 cm,
signed (on the back): G. Münter 1910.
Inv. No. GMS 660

Kandinsky and Erma Bossi at the dinner Table.
1910

Oil on canvas, 95.5 × 125.5 cm,
signed (on the back): Münter.
Inv. No. GMS 780

Still Life in Grey. 1910

Oil on cardboard, 34.2 × 50.2 cm, signed: Münter.
Inv. No. GMS 662
Plate 88

Village Street. 1910

Oil on cardboard, 32.7 × 40.6 cm,
signed: Münter 1910.
On permanent loan from the Gabriele Münter and
Johannes Eichner Foundation.

Child in White. 1910

Oil on cardboard, 44.7 × 33 cm, signed: Münter 10.
Inv. No. GMS 633

Bavarian Landscape with an "Einödshof."
About 1910.

Painting on glass, 14.1 × 21.2 cm, signed: Mü.
Frame painted by Kandinsky.
Inv. No. GMS 735

St. Franz Seraph and St. Julia. About 1910

Painting on glass, 22.8 × 17.5 cm.
Frame painted by Kandinsky.
Inv. No. G 12191

Crucifix in a Landscape. About 1910

Painting on glass, 14.2 × 20.4 cm,
signed (on the back): Gabriele Münter.
Inv. No. G 12190

Murnau from the Water. About 1910

Painting on glass, 9.2 × 14 cm,
signed (on the back): Mü. etwa 1910.
Inv. No. GMS 736

Master-brewer Schöttl of the Anger Brewery, Murnau. About 1910.

Painting on glass, 18.4 × 12.8 cm,
signed (on the back): Gabriele Münter.
Frame painted by Kandinsky.
Inv. No. G 12189

Carts with Straw. 1910–11

Oil on cardboard, 32.9 × 40.8 cm,
signed (on the back): Münter 1911.
Inv. No. GMS 648

Village Street in Winter. 1911

Oil on cardboard, 52.4 × 69 cm,
signed: Münter 1911.
Inv. No. GMS 664
Plate 89

Man at the dinner Table (portrait of Kandinsky). 1911

Oil on cardboard, 51.6 × 68.5 cm, signed: Münter.
Inv. No. 665
Plate 90

Madonna with Christmas Stars. About 1911

Oil on canvas, 92.5 × 70.5 cm, signed: Münter.
Inv. No. G 12206

Still Life with St. George. 1911

Oil on cardboard, 51.1 × 67.9 cm, signed: Münter.
Inv. No. GMS 666
Plate 91

Study with white Spots. 1912

Oil on cardboard, 38.5 × 25.5 cm,
signed: Mü (intertwined) 12.
Inv. No. GMS 667

Still Life with Easter Eggs. 1914

Oil on cardboard, 48.8 × 55.6 cm,
signed: Münter 1914.
Inv. No. GMS 668

Portrait of a Child (Ivan). 1916

Oil on canvas, 45.5 × 38.5 cm, signed: Mü 16.
Inv. No. GMS 669

Color Study (white, green, red). 1916

Oil on cardboard, 25 × 23.5 cm,
signed: Münter 1916.
On permanent loan from the Gabriele Münter and Johannes Eichner Foundation.

Woman musing. 1917

Oil on canvas, 66 × 99.5 cm,
signed: Münter 31. III. 17.
Inv. No. GMS 646
Plate 92

Ill. 1917

Oil on canvas, 78 × 84 cm,
signed: Münter 19, IV. 17.
Inv. No. GMS 782

St. John. 1917

Painting on glass, 12 × 11 cm, signed: Mü.
Inv. No. GMS 737

From the Sixties. 1917

Painting on glass, 12.5 × 9.5 cm, signed: Mü.
Inv. No. GMS 738

Lady with Rose. 1917

Painting on glass, 13 × 9.6 cm, signed: Mü.
Inv. No. GMS 739

House of the Russians [Das Russenhaus]. 1931

Oil on canvas, 42.5 × 57 cm, signed: Münter 1931.
Inv. No. GMS 773

The grey Lake. 1932

Oil on canvas, 54.8 × 65.7 cm,
signed: Münter 1932.
Inv. No. GMS 670

View of the Mountains. 1934

Oil on canvas, 46.6 × 55.5 cm,
signed: Münter 1934.
Inv. No. G 12944
Plate 93

Peonies and orange Lily. 1956

Oil on paper, 61 × 43 cm,
signed: BB 13/56 Mü (intertwined).
Inv. No. GMS 748
Plate 94

Jean Bloé Niestlé

Born 16 August 1884 in Neuchâtel, Switzerland,
died 9 February 1942 in Antony (Seine). He attended art school in 1903, in Nuremberg. In 1904
he studied with Moritz Heymann in Munich, met
Jules Pascin, and took lessons from Berlepsch in
Planegg, near Munich. In about 1906 he became
friends with Franz Marc, and in 1910 moved to
Sindelsdorf, where Marc lived. Bernhard Koehler
acquired a series of his paintings. One of his paintings was included in the first "Blue Rider" exhibition. Early in 1914 he moved to Seeshaupt, where
Koehler had placed a house at his disposal. In February 1918 he fell seriously ill with influenza of
the head, with incurable consequences. He moved
to Paris in 1937 and later to Chatou (Seine-et-
Oise). In 1939 he fled from the German troops in
the neighborhood of Nantes, and the next year
moved to Antony (Seine).

Water Pipit. 1909

Oil on canvas, 65 × 90 cm, signed: J. B. Niestlé 09.
Bernhard Koehler Bequest, 1965.
Inv. No. G 13337
Plate 95

Cat on the Prowl. 1910

Oil on canvas, 51 × 56.5 cm, signed: J. B. Niestlé 10.
Bernhard Koehler Bequest, 1965.
Inv. No. G 13336
Plate 97

Migrating Starlings. 1910

Oil on canvas, 90,5 × 151 cm,
signed: J. B. Niestlé 10.
Bernhard Koehler Bequest, 1965.
Inv. No. G 13338
Plate 96

Alexander von Salzmann

Born 1873 (?) in Tiflis, died about 1914 in Paris.
He studied at the Munich Academy in Stuck's class
in 1898, and became a member of the artists' union,
"Phalanx," in 1901–4. He was a collaborator of
the Munich magazine *Jugend.* From 1910 he lived
in Hellerau, near Dresden. He went to Paris
around 1912 and married there.

In front of the Castle [Vor dem Schloß]. 1910.

Tempera, 50.5 × 72 cm, signed: AS (intertwined)/10.
Inv. No. G 14251

E. Schiemann

Dates unknown; Russian artist and craftsman,
friend of the "Blue Riders."

Grotesque I. About 1910

Watercolor, 35 × 35.8 cm, signed: E. Schiemann.
From Gabriele Münter's collection.
Inv. No. GMS 749

Grotesque II. About 1910

Watercolor, 14.1 × 18 cm, signed (on passe-par-
tout): E. Schiemann.
From Gabriele Münter's collection.
Inv. No. GMS 750

Design for the cover of the *Almanach Der Blaue Reiter*. About 1911
(using a motif of Franz Marc's)

Painted on silk, 23.2 × 18.5 cm.
From Gabriele Münter's collection.
Inv. No. GMS 784

Arnold Schönberg

Born 13 September 1874 in Vienna, died 13 July 1951 in Los Angeles. Self-taught musician and painter. Three of his paintings were included in the first "Blue Rider" exhibition. He published the composition *"Herzgewächse* (M. Maeterlinck) for soprano, celeste, harmonium, and harp" in the *Almanach Der Blaue Reiter*.

Red Eyes. About 1910

Oil on cardboard, 32.2 × 24.6 cm,
signed: Arnold Schönberg Mai 1910.
On permanent loan from the Schönberg Estate.
Plate 98

Hands. 1910

Oil on canvas, 33.3 × 22.2 cm.
On permanent loan from the Schönberg Estate.

Marianne von Werefkin

Born 29 August 1860 in Tula, Russia, died 6 February 1938 in Ascona. She took her first lessons in Lublin. In 1883 she studied with Prjanishnikov, a teacher at the Moscow Art School, and from 1886 was a private pupil of Ilja Rjepin in St. Petersburg. She met Jawlensky in 1891, and in 1897 went with him to Munich. She was in Paris in about 1901–2, and subsequently went back to Munich. The NKVM was founded in her drawing room in 1909, and she participated in its three exhibitions. She also took part in the *Sonderbund* exhibition in Cologne, in the first German *Herbstsalon* in 1913, and in the "Blue Rider" exhibition organized by *Der Sturm* in 1913. In 1914 she went with Jawlensky to Saint-Prex on the Lake of Geneva, and in 1917 accompanied him to Zürich. She lived in Ascona from 1918 until her death.

Portrait of Alexej von Jawlensky. 1896

Oil on canvas, 42 × 24.5 cm.
Inv. No. G 13582

Self-portrait I. About 1908

Oil on cardboard, 51 × 34 cm.
Donated by Gabriele Münter.
Inv. No. 13144
Plate 99

Interior with seated Couple. About 1910

Mixed media, 37.3 × 27.5 cm, signed: M. W.
From Gabriele Münter's collection.
Inv. No. GMS 712
Plate 100

Washerwomen. About 1910

Tempera on cardboard, 50.5 × 64 cm.
From Gabriele Münter's collection.
Inv. No. GMS 711

LIST OF PLATES

169